# LEONARDO DA VINCI

## Geologic Representations in

## THE VIRGIN AND CHILD WITH ST. ANNE

### Ann C. Pizzorusso

Published in the United States by: Da Vinci Press New York, New York 10011
email: davincipress@gmail.com
Cover design: Francesco Filippini
Design artist: Francesco Filippini
ISBN: 978-1-940613-04-8
Library of Congress Control Number: 2020924633

1. Leonardo da Vinci 2. Italy 3. Geology 4. Dolomites 5. Art 6. Art History 7. Art Criticism 8. Virgin and Child with St. Anne 9. Painting 10. Louvre 11. Renaissance 12. Pizzorusso.

Dedicated To

Carlo Pedretti
The *paterfamilias* of Leonardo Da Vinci Studies

and

John Sanders
Geologist

# INTRODUCTORY NOTE TO READER

When Leonardo da Vinci left Florence for Milan in 1482, he spent considerable time exploring the Alps. In 1500 he arrived in the Veneto area and saw the Dolomites (shown in red), mountains which are a part of the northestern Alps.

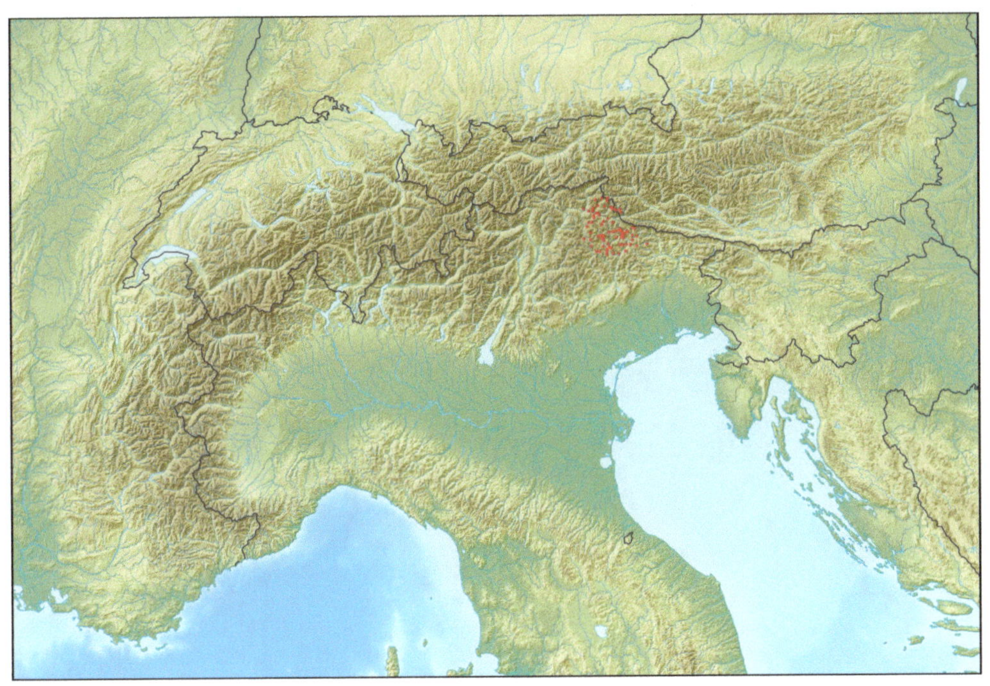

He would have been awestruck upon seeing the three peaks of Lavaredo.

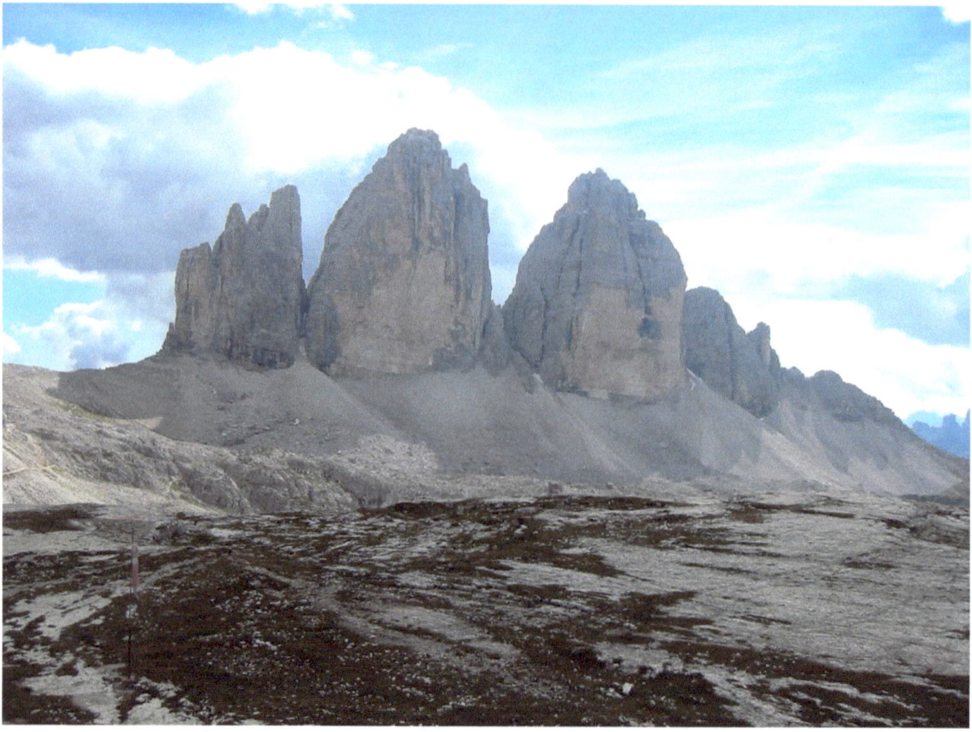

He would have noted how the tree's golden hue blended with the gray mountains and how the clouds and mists provided a diffused, soft light.

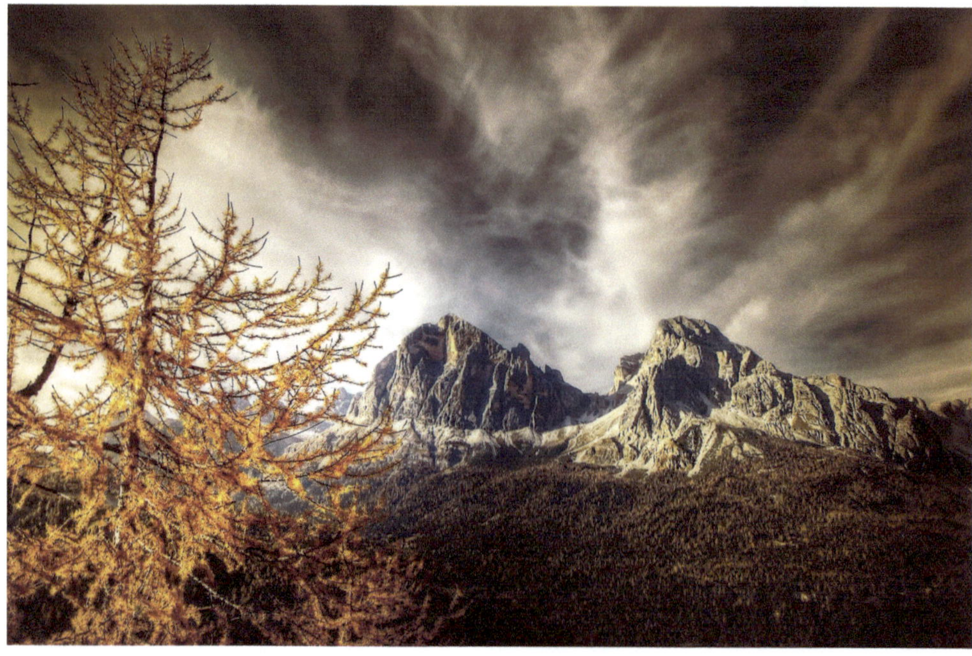

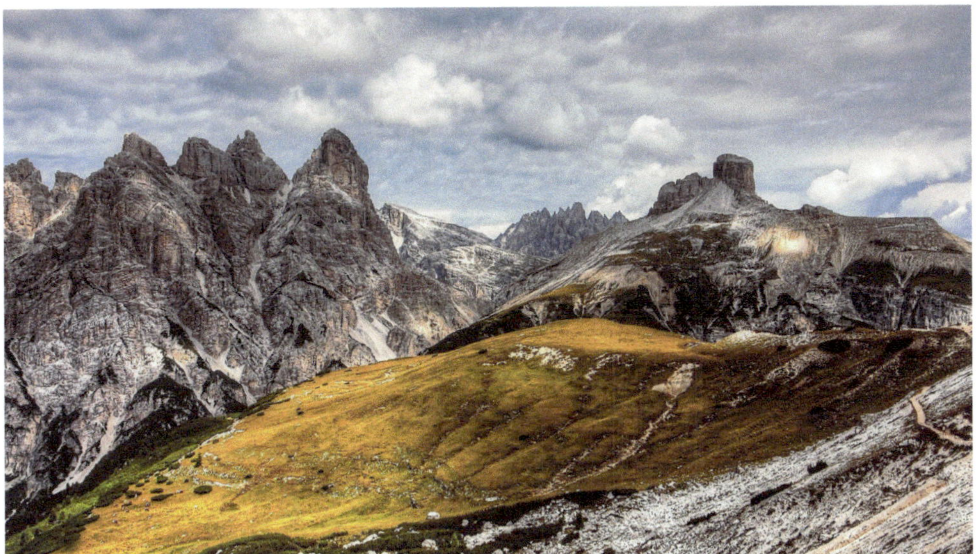

Since the mountains are divided by meadows, Leonardo would have noticed the different topographic features and color variations associated with each.

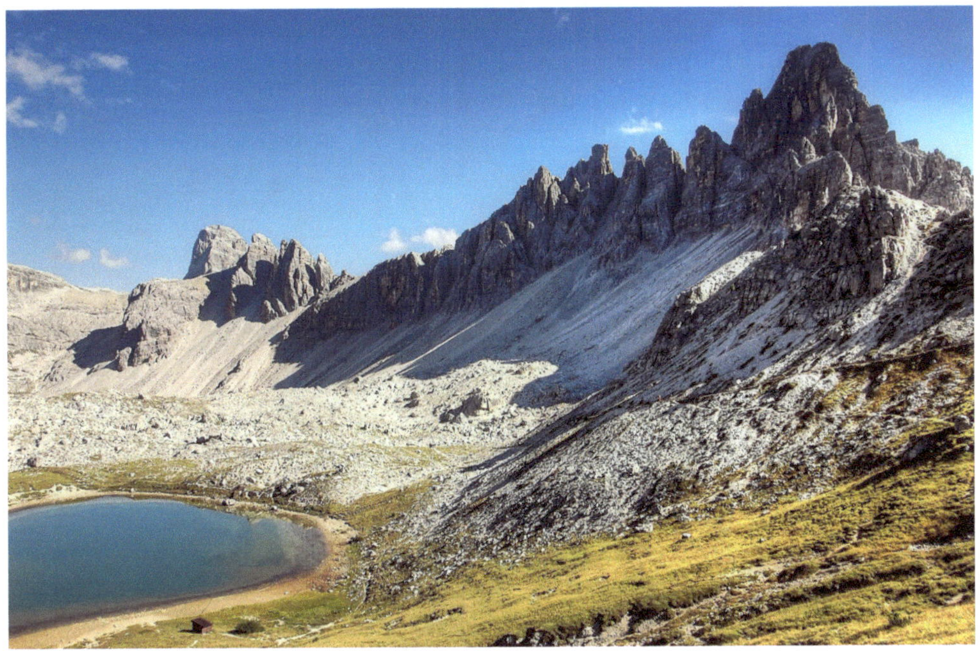

Between the mountains and meadows, isolated lakes, formed by melting glaciers, are another distinctive feature of this area.

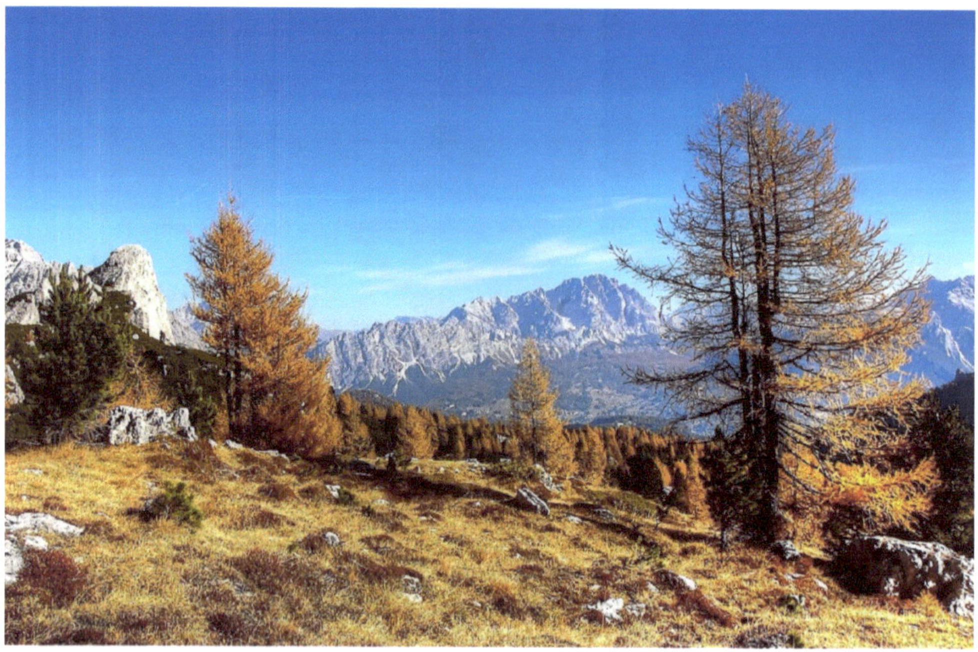

As an artist, Leonardo would have been impressed by the harmony of colors displayed in the area in autumn.

Now that you have in mind the actual topography, and have seen it in different seasons, it will be easy to understand how the geology of the Dolomites influenced Leonardo.

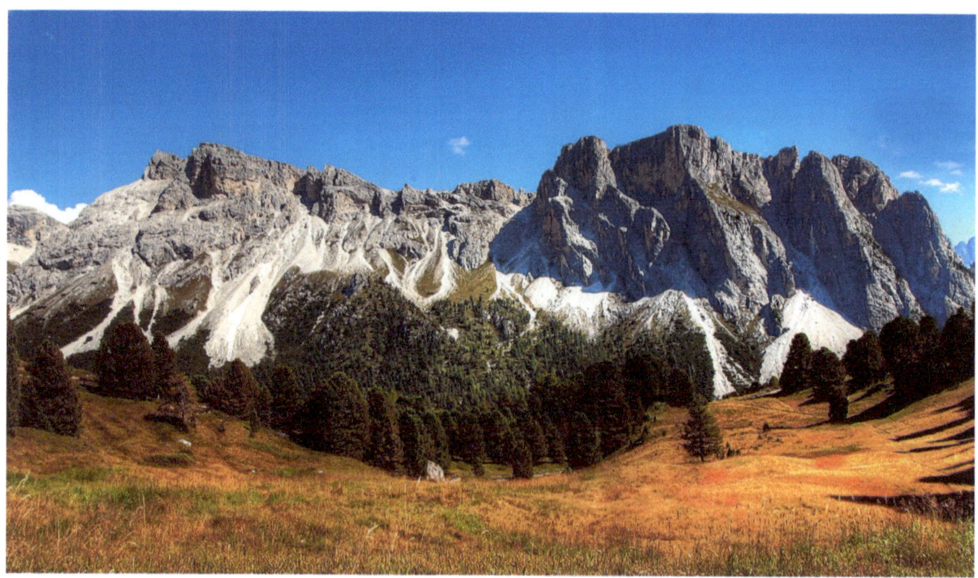

And here is Leonardo's painting, the Virgin and Child with St. Anne.
Does it look familiar?
So now, we can start the story.

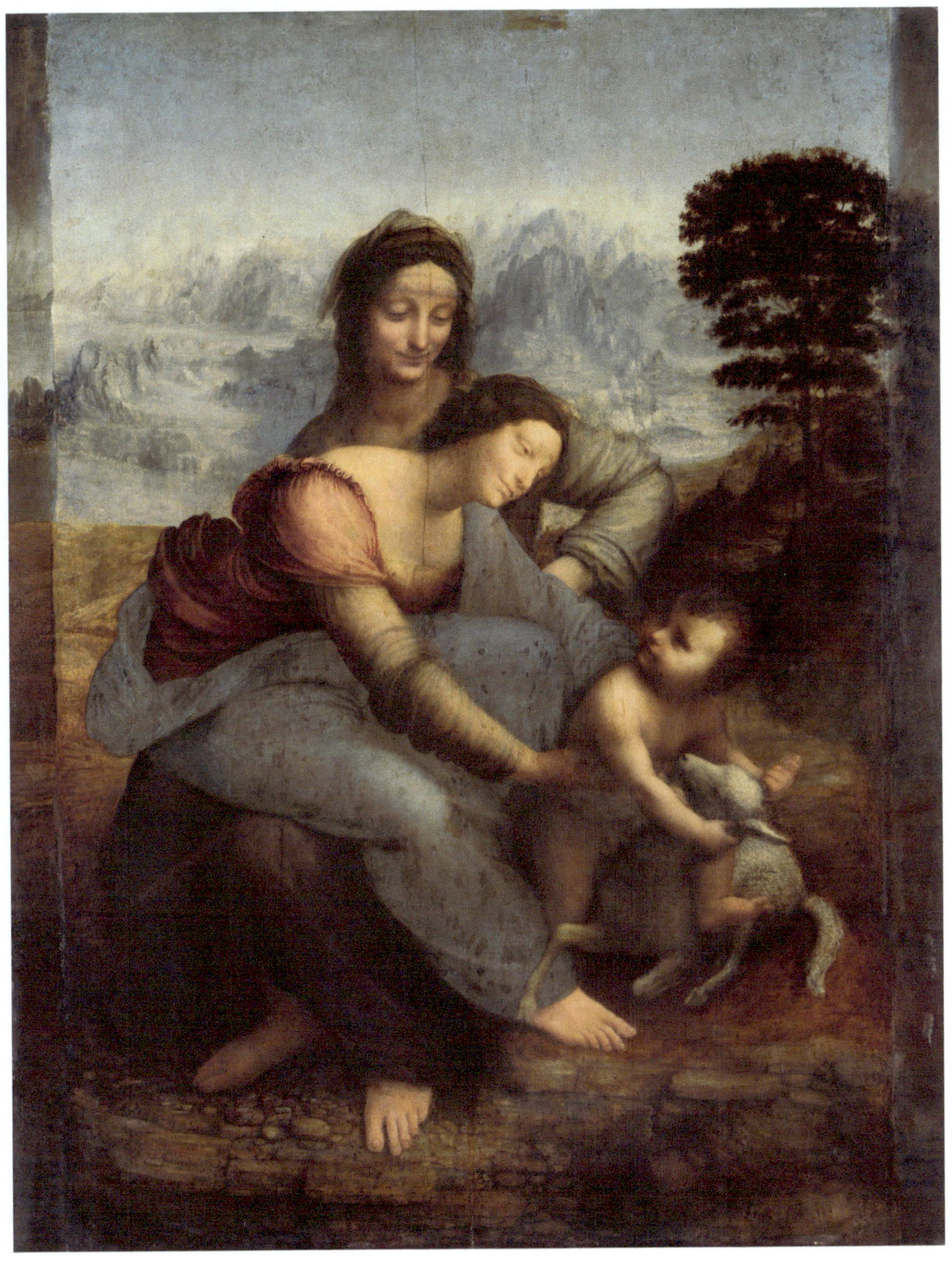

Leonardo da Vinci's Virgin and Child with St. Anne (St. Anne) has been the subject of speculation by historians and occultists ever since it was painted circa 1501-1517.[1] In it, the Christ child is shown clutching a sacrificial lamb, symbol of His Passion, while the Virgin reaches over to restrain Him and her mother, St. Anne, looks upon them wistfully.

Art critics, psychiatrists and medical doctors are among the many who have been fascinated with this painting. Each has interpreted it to reflect his own profession: Bernard Berenson, the art critic, disliked the composition because it appeared as if St. Anne was crouching,[2] Sigmund Freud found deep psychological implications in the representation of the Virgin and St. Anne,[3] and a medical doctor imagined seeing ensanguined embryos in the pebbles below St. Anne's foot.[4] According to Patrice Boussel: "Many consider the St. Anne a treasure trove of esoterica and occult wonders; some see in it the expanding cosmos and an all-embracing system of beliefs".[5]

What a marvelous picture to elicit comments from experts in such diverse disciplines. Yet, since it is set in the Dolomites, mountains which are part of the Alps in northeastern Italy, it seems only right to analyze the painting's geology. As will be shown, the geologic formations in the picture are depicted with Leonardo's trademark accuracy, and thus, are identifiable.[6] More importantly, the geology provides a scientific basis for addressing much of the speculation and interpretation which has been lavished on this painting.

Some background on Leonardo's travels and his interest in geology is needed to place the St. Anne in perspective. In 1482, when Leonardo was thirty, he left Florence to work for Ludovico Sforza in Milan. There, he became fascinated with the geology of the Alps. He spent much time in the mountains observing natural objects and recording them in his notebooks, most notably the Manuscripts of France, the Codex Atlanticus and later in his life, the Codex Leceister. His notebooks present his views on a variety of geologic topics[7] both his written and sketched entries allowed him to memorialize his field observations precisely. As a result, his landscape paintings consistently portrayed nature accurately, a trait which few other artists valued or could replicate. The St. Anne, is a classic example of the geologic realism which is an immutable characteristic of Leonardo's style; it was sacrosanct and is today, a vitally important factor to consider when evaluating works which might be attributed to him. His geologic observations and love of landscapes compelled him to counsel other artists. In his various notebooks, he details the best way to depict mountains, mists and other natural objects.[8] He also described a painter's power. "The painter can call into being the essences of animals of all kinds, of plants, fruits, landscapes, rolling plains, crumbling mountains...places sweet and delightful with meadows of many- colored flowers bent by the gentle motion of the wind which turns back to look at them".[9] Leonardo was very exacting in his portrayal of the natural environment. He objected to the Renaissance practice of using some vague, inaccurate landscapes, whose only purpose was to act as a backdrop for the more important human figures. He went on to criticize the "very bad landscapes"[10] of Botticelli and continued by stating that "the painter is not well rounded who does not have an equally keen interest in all things within the compass of painting".[11] Leonardo's sketches show that he had long been interested in the idea of portraying figures sitting and intertwined in ergonomically complex positions. After much trial and error, he decided to place them rock ledges, perfect for supporting their weight while assuring that his convoluted configurations would appear natural.

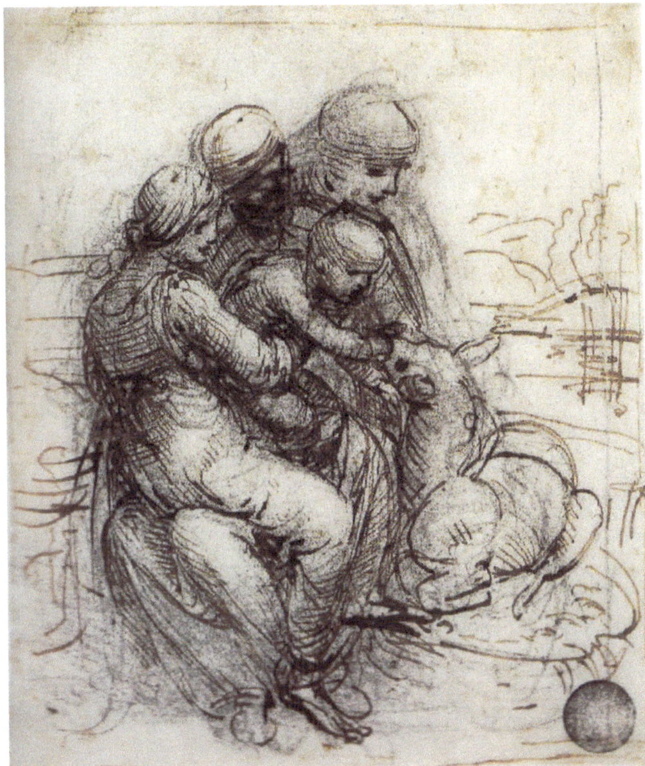

Fig. 1. Leonardo da Vinci, St. Anne, the Virgin and Child playing with a lamb. Note how he works to intertwine the figures so there is a sensation of dynamic fluidity, while at the same time realistic stability. Gallerie dell'Accademia, Venice. Wikimedia commons.

In da Vinci's unfinished Adoration of the Magi, 1481 (Fig. 2.), the Blessed Virgin is sitting upon a rock ledge with the infant Jesus reaching out to one of the Magi. Her feet are positioned on a lower stratified rock ledge. Here, Leonardo uses a stair-step configuration of rocks (which extend upward to form the base of the tree) on which he placed objects and figures to create a focal point of immense complexity. While we can see expanses of dark colored paint, these areas would provide the colored base upon which he would define the rock ledge and the rocky area in the foreground to include the stratified rock and pebbles we see in his other paintings. The fractured strata would also provide a safe space for the Virgin and Child as they would be protected by the rock wall behind them. He would continue to experiment with landscape and composition to eventually produce the grotto we see in the Virgin of the Rocks (Louvre).

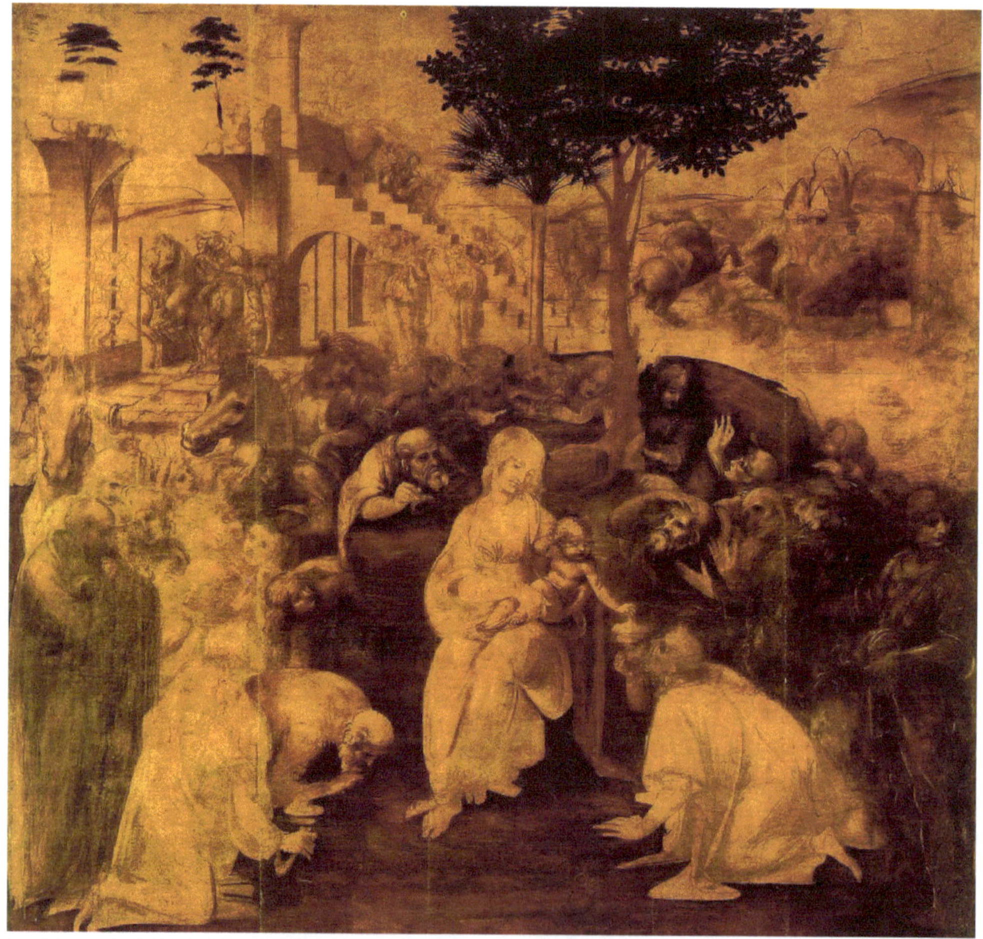

Fig. 2. Leonardo da Vinci, Adoration of the Magi, 1481, Uffizi Gallery, Florence, Italy. Wikimedia commons.

Leonardo was working on the idea of a figure(s) sitting and intertwined, but it took him years to execute it to his satisfaction. While the idea in the Adoration of the Magi started simply, with just the Virgin and Child, over the ensuing years, it evolved into one which was infinitely more complex as he sought, in the St. Anne to place three figures and a lamb together on rock ledges; with all four in motion. Considering the complexity of the configuration, it is no wonder he prepared numerous sketches. The most notable of which, was the Burlington House Cartoon (National Gallery, London), the model for the painting which generated much awe when it was viewed by the public for the first time. (Fig. 3.).

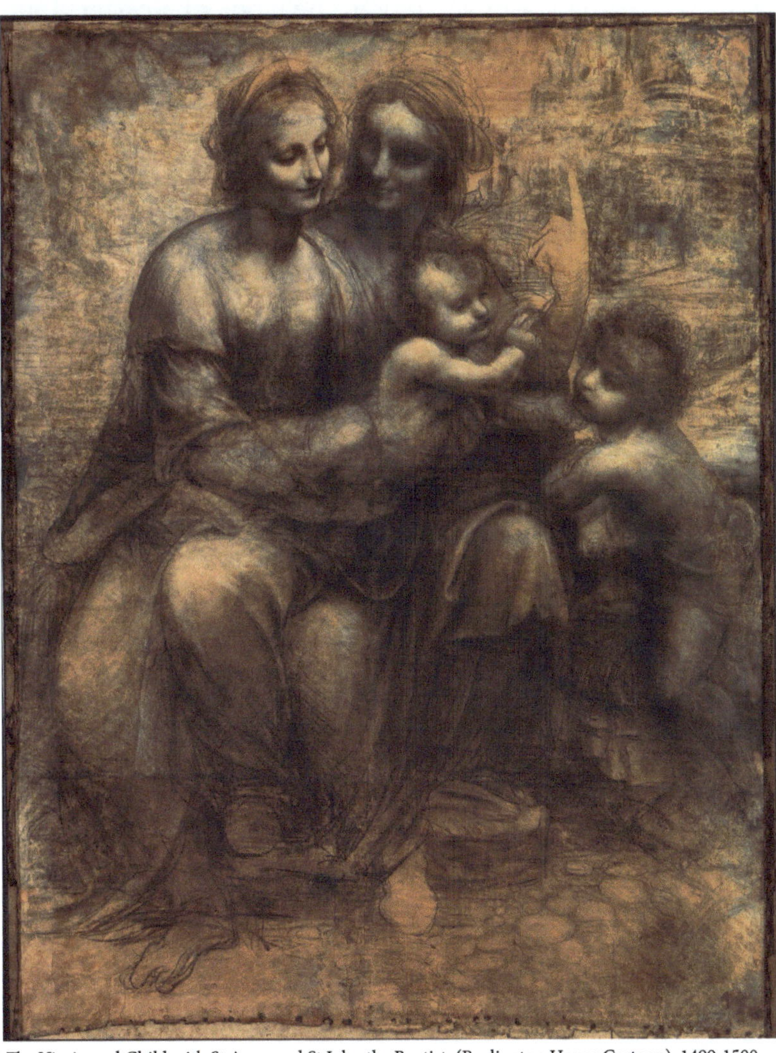

Fig. 3. Leonardo da Vinci, The Virgin and Child with St Anne and St John the Baptist, (Burlington House Cartoon), 1499-1500, National Gallery, London. Wikimedia commons.

The exact date of the St. Anne's creation has not been determined, but art historians date it between 1501 and 1517, keeping in mind that Leonardo worked on it for years yet never completed it. According to Vasari, the St. Anne was commissioned by the monks of Santissima Annunziata in Florence for their high altar. Leonardo expert, Carlo Pedretti finds no evidence for this.[12] And, according to James Beck,[13] the St. Anne, like the Mona Lisa, remained with Leonardo until his death. The St. Anne, 1501-1517 was painted after the Virgin of the Rocks, Louvre, 1483-86 and the Mona Lisa, 1503-06, all of which exhibit Leonardo's trademark geologic accuracy.[14] Leonardo visited the Alpine regions of the Veneto in the early months of 1500.15 He was also writing about geology in the Codex Leicester, 1506- 1510 and memorializing his observations in various sketches which portray an array of various geologic formations. Art historians agree that the St. Anne was executed by Leonardo with the help of assistants. However, x-rays indicate that the entire under- drawing was completed by Leonardo.[16] Art historians also agree that the landscape was completed entirely by Leonardo.[17] This is an accurate conclusion because it exhibits the geologic detail that is Leonardo's trademark style.

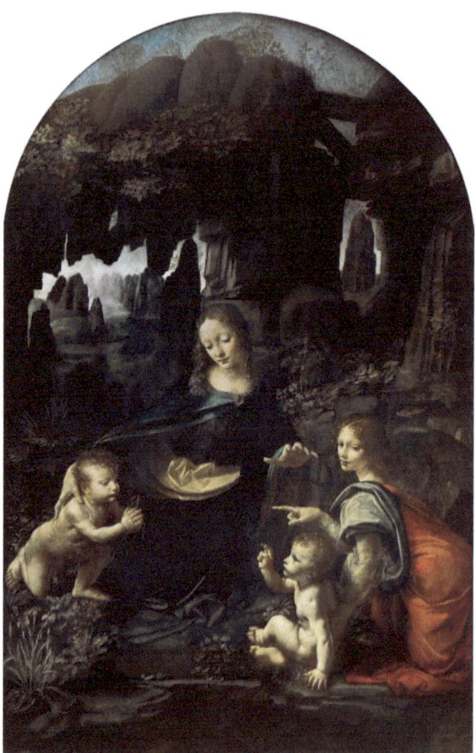

Fig. 4. Leonardo da Vinci, Virgin of the Rocks, 1483-86, Louvre, Paris. Wikimedia commons.

The St. Anne is reminiscent of the Virgin of the Rocks (Fig. 4.) because of the placement of a group of figures in a natural landscape. And, it resembles the Mona Lisa (Fig. 5.) because of the panoramic vista filled with geologic formations. As he did with his other paintings, Leonardo made many preparatory sketches for the St. Anne. The extant sketches include representations of heads, arms, drapery, botany (see Appendix B for a discussion of the identification of the tree) and of course, the geologic features that he would include in his final painting. He struggled until he found the right composition that would allow him to depict figures in pyramidal structure, an extremely difficult endeavor. He was able to find the perfect vehicle for achieving this by using a rock ledge, on which he placed the dynamic twisting and turning figures, thus creating an ideal composition.

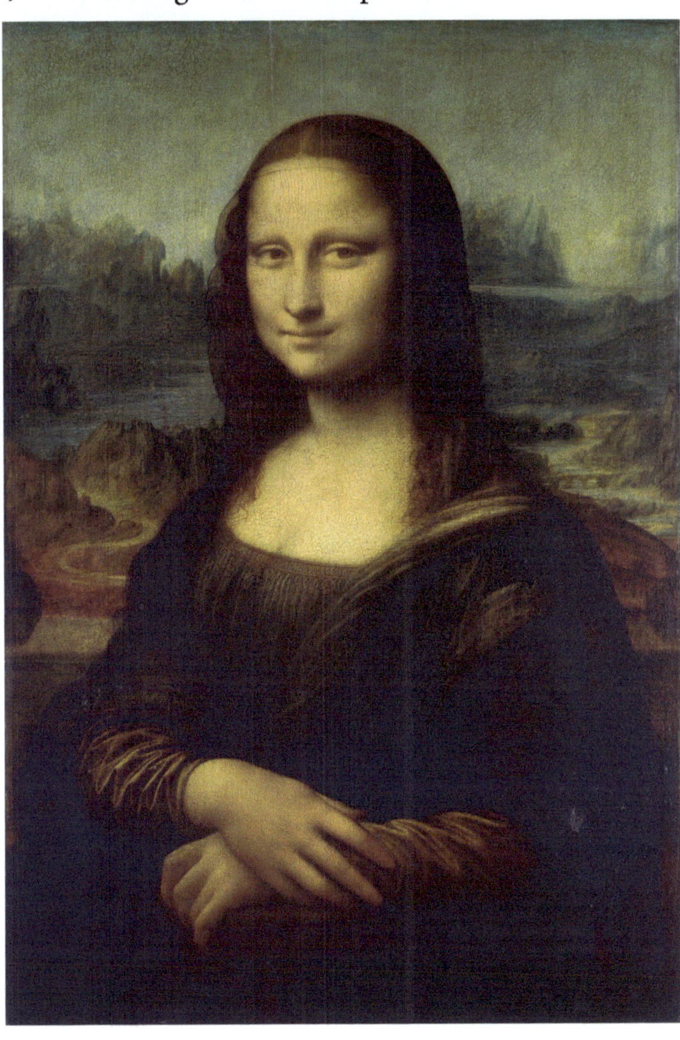

Fig. 5. Leonardo da Vinci, Mona Lisa, 1503-06, Louvre, Paris. Wikimedia commons.

The St. Anne is compelling because it flawlessly creates a pyramidal structure of intertwined figures in an equally complex geologic environment. The St. Anne is divided into two sections; the intimate foreground valley, with its warm, earth-tone colors, adjacent to the panoramic, majestic, massifs in the background, portrayed with cool blues and grays (Fig. 6.). Leonardo uses a variety of painting techniques to give us a sense of space and perspective. James Beck notes the use of chiaroscuro in the painting, "Larger areas of shadow and light are laid out softly, operating on each other as if the artist has gone beyond the point of finishing. Most contours are obliterated, and the isolating of forms takes place in the eye of the beholder rather than on the painted surface."[18] The colors of the background are cool, accurately depicting the natural and atmospheric conditions present: the gray of the mountains, the blue-white of the glacier, and the greenish gray mists accumulating in the mountain valleys. Because it depicts a landscape above the tree line, no trees are present. However, at a much lower altitude, a large ash tree, which is discussed in detail in Appendix B, is shown. Art critics have imagined that the tree was a symbol of the wooden cross upon which Christ would be sacrificed. Kenneth Clark expresses his impression of the background as Leonardo giving us "The sense of the world as a planet, seen from a point of distance at which human life is no longer visible, is given final expression in the background of the Virgin and Child and St. Anne."[19]

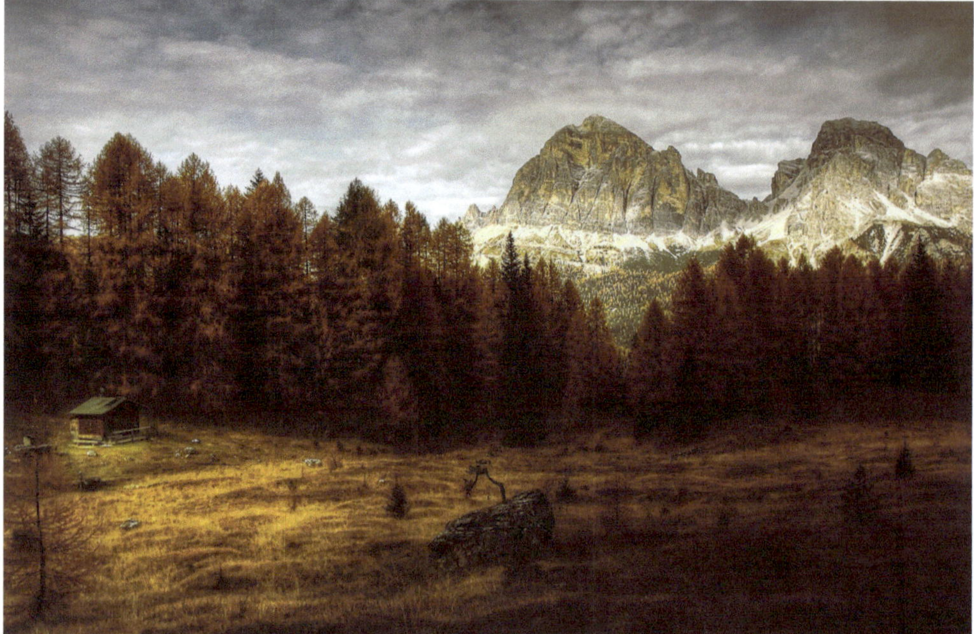

Fig. 6. View of Dolomites landscape with mountains in the background and meadows in the foreground. Wikimedia commons.

The foreground of the picture has, however, caused the most controversy. In discussing the figure of the Virgin, Carlo Pedretti, states that "Critics have often wondered why Leonardo should have abandoned the most satisfactory Classical sense of balance achieved in the London Burlington House Cartoon (Fig.3.) in favor of a pose that has always been taken as conveying a sense of uneasiness."[20] Bernard Berenson summarized his dismay with Leonardo's treatment of St. Anne as follows; "Seated on no visible or inferable support, she (St. Anne) in turn on her left knee sustained the restless weight of a daughter as heavy as herself."[21]

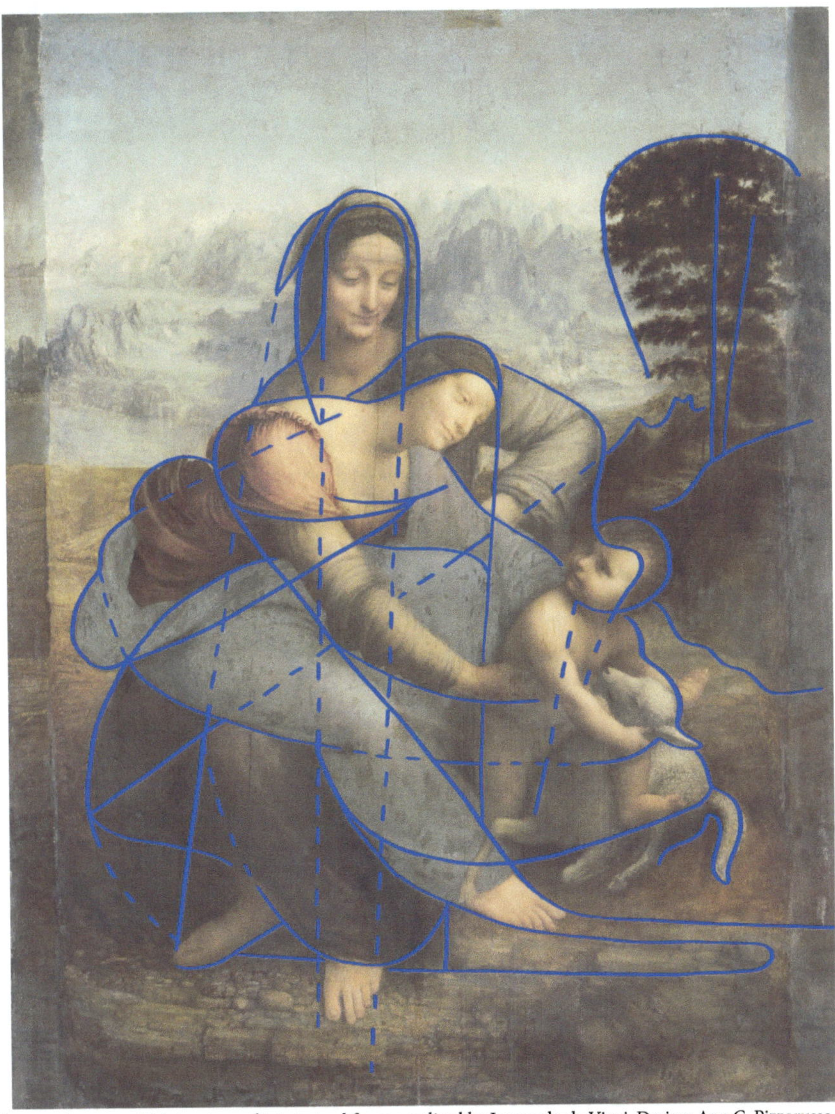

Fig. 7. Outline of the complex pyramidal structure of intertwined figures realized by Leonardo da Vinci. Design: Ann C. Pizzorusso

Had Berenson known his geology, he would have seen that St. Anne is not suspended in mid-air, but rather, seated on a natural rock ledge, the outline of which is shown in Fig. 8. We can trace it by looking at the lower left-hand corner of the picture, where St. Anne's two feet are resting on bedded rock which has been weathered to a brownish coppery color. The Virgin's foot rests on another ledge, higher in the picture. The lamb's back feet rest on yet another, slightly ledge. Another ledge rises near the Child's right hand. At the shoulder of the Child another ledge rises and recedes into the background, toward the trees. By using these stair-step rock ledges, the individual centers of gravity of each figure are such that they are stable, allowing them to turn and reach out to one another, thus creating a scene imbued with a marvelous fluidity of movement.

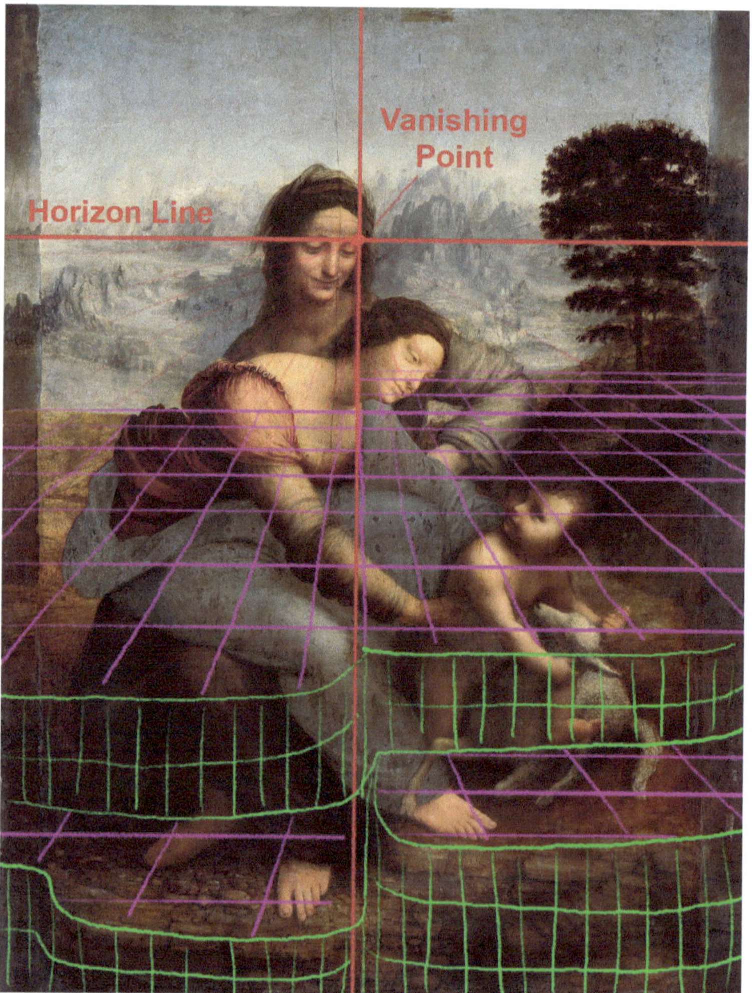


Fig. 8. Outline of the stair-step rock strata on which Leonardo placed his figures. © Ann C. Pizzorusso 2021

Carlo Pedretti explains that the seated position of St. Anne and the Virgin can be understood by looking at the folds of their garments and the inferred position of their legs beneath.[22] According to Pedretti, Leonardo prepared many sketches for the garments so that they would accurately reflect the position of the body beneath. Leonardo also experimented with many compositions of people balancing themselves in various positions to arrive at an accurate depiction of musculature and pose.

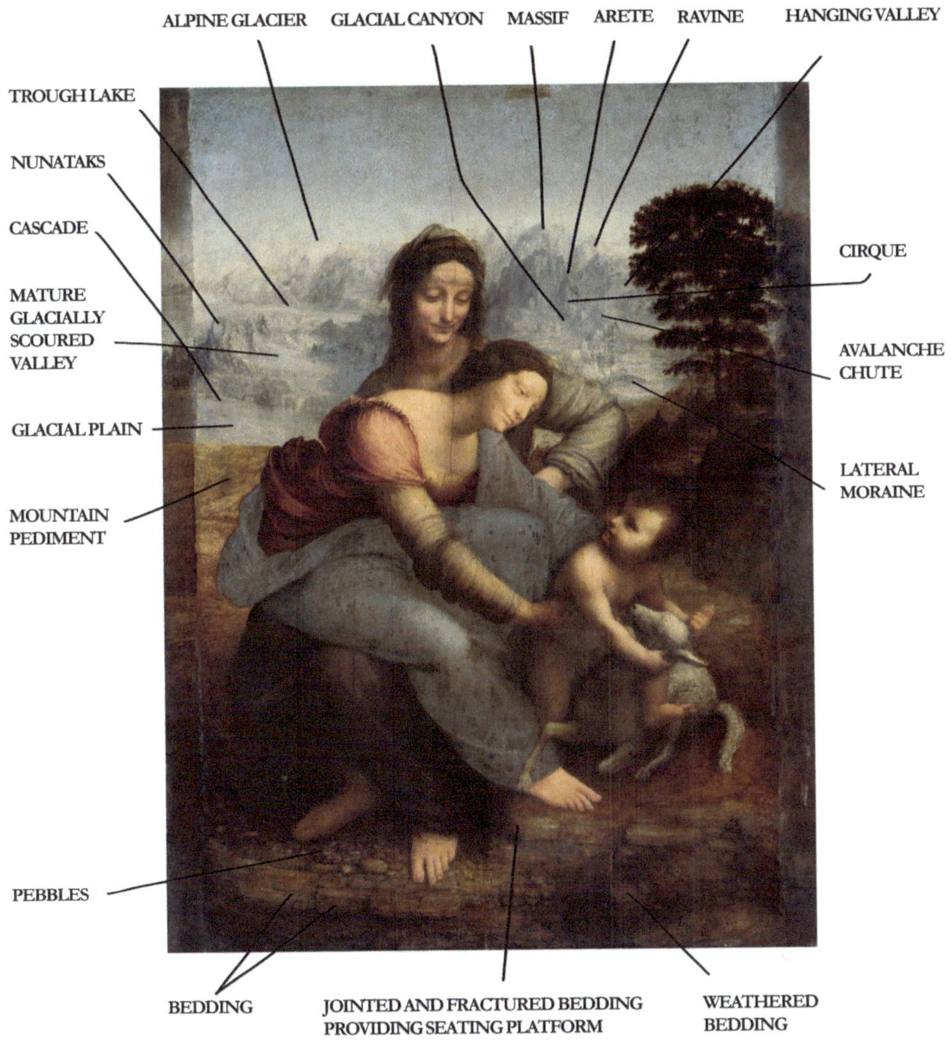


Fig. 9. Identification of geologic formations in the Virgin and Child and St. Anne, 1501-1517, Louvre, Paris. © Ann C. Pizzorusso 2021

In Fig. 9 we can see how Leonardo was inspired by the Dolomites. Because of his artistic prowess, he captured the geologic formations so accurately that we are able to identify them readily. The massifs are ancient coral reefs which rose up from the bottom of the ancient Tethys Ocean which once covered the area some 250 million years ago. In the background, to the right of St. Anne's head are weathered rock pinnacles. These pinnacles are so common in the Alps that there are numerous descriptive names for their various forms in the Italian geologic dictionary. They are hard, durable rocks which have withstood the weathering effects of glacial scour, wind, water and gravity which together result in erosion. Canyons, on the other hand, formed when glaciers scoured away less resistant rock. Ravines, arêtes, hanging valleys, avalanche chutes, cirques and terminal moraines are all characteristic of Alpine glacial geology and are depicted in the painting. In the background, to the left of St. Anne's head is an alpine glacier, one which nestles in the valleys of mountainous terrain. Today there is only one glacier in the Dolomites, the Marmolada, with a trough lake called Fedaia below it. When a glacier which existed in the past moved to lower elevations, it eroded a wide swath of earth and eventually melted, creating a mature scoured valley. The jagged peaks emerging from the ground, along the side of the mature scoured valley are called nunatuks. The accumulation of rocky material deposited at the point of furthest advance of a glacier is called a terminal moraine. Since the rocks in the Dolomites are rich in calcium and magnesium carbonate, they can be altered by the effects of wind, water and chemical leaching, resulting in a complex and beautifully sculpted landscape. A broad surface created by the scouring effect of a glacier and subsequent erosion of the surface to smooth it out is called a glacial plain. Subglacial streams typically flow beneath the glacier and can emerge from the glacier portal. Thus, glacier melt water makes its way down the scoured valley and cascades over the terminal moraine. Leonardo depicts the cascade not only as a waterfall descending from a precipice but as a series of streams emerging from fractures in the rocks. The churning waters at the base of the cascade are created through a meticulously executed series of circular eddies painted in a creamy white color, resembling foam. Further out from the falls, the water calmly settles into the glacially scoured valley forming a lake. This attention to detail imparts realism to the scene, even if it is in a minute area of the background. The textured surface in the foreground, depicted in a warm brown color is a mountain pediment, a rough, uneven deposit of rocks and glacial debris. This is, in fact, a typical landscape of the

Dolomites, one where the dramatically high massifs are separated by meadows. The horizontal lines represent the various layers or beds of rock, possibly weathered limestone or dolostone which are painstakingly depicted. The rock has been subject to erosional forces such as wind and water and has broken apart or fractured along bedding planes and joints, the planes of least resistance. The vertical lines represent joints and fractures formed naturally during pressure changes induced by uplift and erosion and by the force of water and ice which would cause the rock to break. Once the rock is split open, water infiltrates the cavities and silica (carried in by the groundwater or present in the parent rock) starts to crystallize into colorful pebbles of chalcedony and agates. These can be seen near the foot of St. Anne. Natural erosional of bedding planes and high angle joints formed an ascending natural rock ledge. Indeed, this ledge is configured in a stair step like manner, rising from St. Anne's feet to a higher level to accommodate Mary's foot to still a higher level for the lamb. It continues to rise behind the lamb and Jesus, until it recedes into the background. The bedded rock in the foreground is characteristic of Leonardo's style (see the foreground in the Virgin of the Rocks, Louvre). Considering the geology of the Dolomites, the rocks depicted could be strata of bedded carbonates with some silicified agate pebbly lenses. Da Vinci's designs and field notes show that he had been observing the weathering patterns of stratified rock, portraying the rock's texture, color and formation realistically. Thus, the strata he shows in the foreground, can be seen to have been subject to considerable erosion by wind and water.

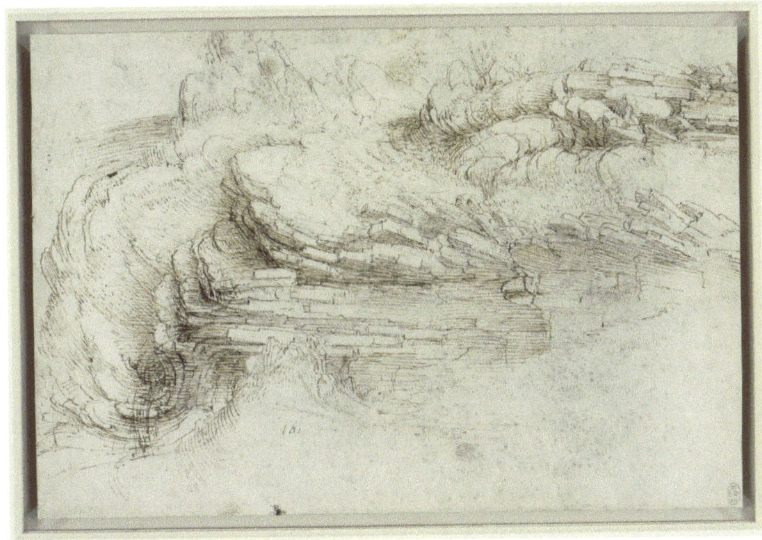

Fig. 10. Leonardo da Vinci, Outcrop of Stratified Rock, c.1510, (RL 12394) Royal Collection Trust © Her Majesty Queen Elizabeth II, 2020.

The pebbles in the foreground are a product of weathering (rocks being eroded into rounded shapes by wind and water). These pebbles give a great deal of insight into Leonardo's artistic and scientific interests at the time, for he has portrayed, with astonishing accuracy, jaspers and banded agates. Leonardo purposely painted them with the muted, dull colors that they would have as a result of being weathered significantly[23]. Thus, we can see the inner mottled and marbled contours, but subtly, as through a hazy outer shell.

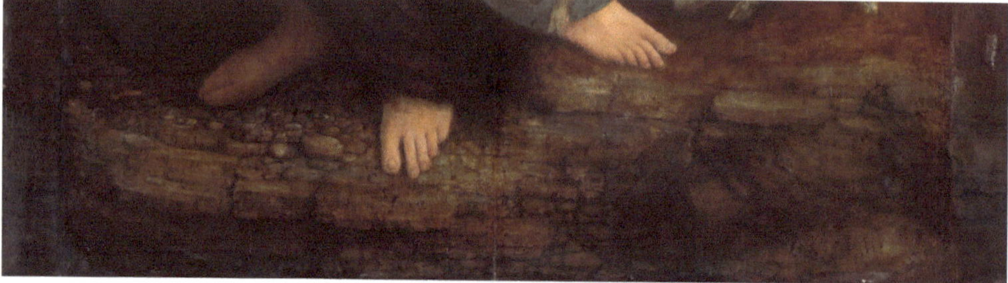

Fig. 11. Virgin and St. Anne with Child, Louvre, detail of stratified rock and pebbles. Wikimedia commons.

As for an unsettling interpretation, Raymond Stites states "Between the feet of the St. Anne in this pool[24] there is a distinctly recognizable embryo (fetus) of two or three months, with a number of similar forms, each smaller than the last, which seem to be a row of tinier fetuses...and what seems to be the end of an umbilical cord emerging from between two rocks of the pool."[25] Stites confirms his impression by quoting from the following letter: "Dr. George W. Corner, Director of the Carnegie Institution of Washington, Department of Embryology in Baltimore, wrote me in 1953, that while he, himself, could not agree with my interpretation (author's note: the presence of "fetuses"), one of his colleagues thought the pebble bore resemblance to "a sheep fetus." He also wrote "either the appearance of organic structure is fortuitous, or that Leonardo da Vinci was indeed indulging in a very subtle sort of surrealism."[26] Carlo Pedretti indicates however, that the concept of a bloody embryo dropped among the rocks was an insult to Leonardo's sense of decorum.[27]

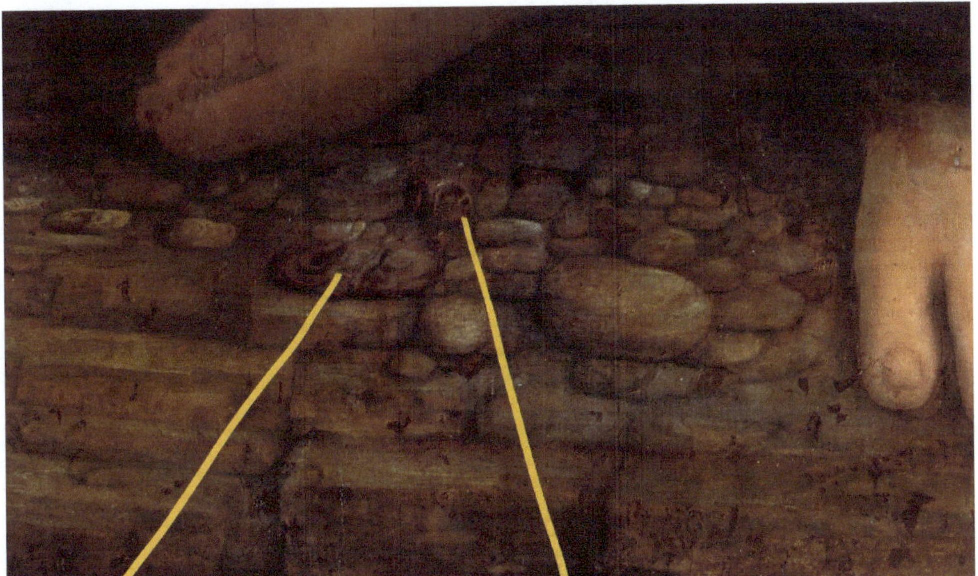

Fig. 12 Virgin and Child with St. Anne, Louvre. Note pebbles of agate and jasper identified by Raymond Stites as embryos. Wikimedia commons.

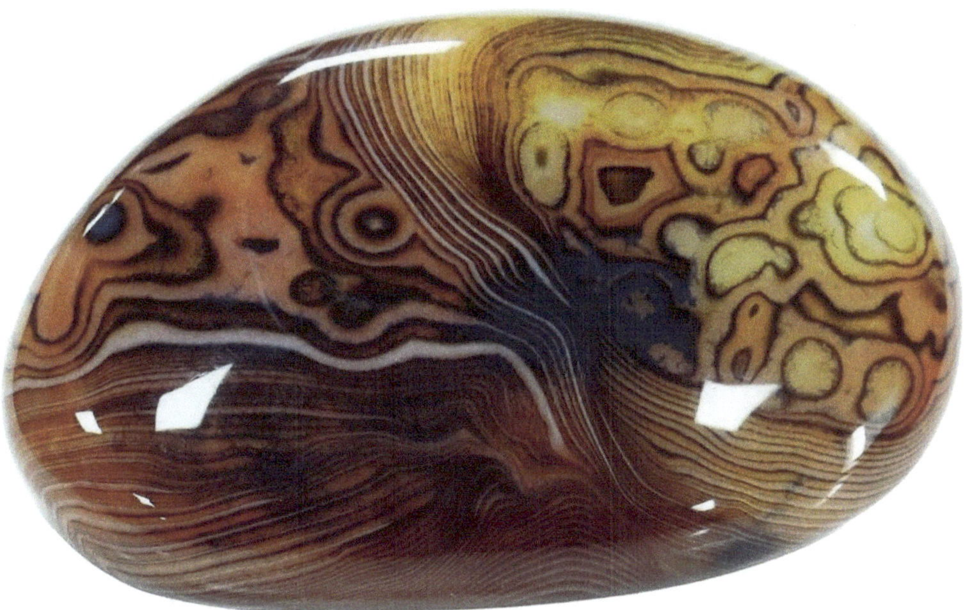

Fig. 13. Banded agate. Wikimedia commons.

While claims of seeing embryos within the pebbles seem to be bizarre, those who see images in these stones cannot be faulted, for it is commonplace. It is called pareidolia, which is the perception of a recognizable image or meaningful pattern where none exists or is intended, such as faces on the surface of the moon. The term mimetolithic applies precisely to a pattern created by rocks in which recognizable forms are seen on or within them, yet caused by weathering and erosion. When Leonardo described methods a painter could use for inspiration, he actually described both pareidolic and mimetolithic patterns in a detailed notebook entry. "I will not refrain from setting among these precepts a new device for consideration which, although it may appear trivial and almost ludicrous, is nevertheless of great utility in arousing the mind to various inventions. And this is, that if you look at any walls spotted with various stains, or with a mixture of different kinds of stones, if you are about to invent some scene you will be able to see in it a resemblance to various different landscapes adorned with mountains, rivers, rocks, trees, plains, wide valleys, and various groups of hills. You will also be able to see divers combats and figures in quick movement, and strange expression of faces, and outlandish costumes, and an infinite number of things which you can then reduce into separate and well- conceived forms. With such walls and blends of different stones it comes about as it does with the sound of bells, in whose clanging you may discover every name and word you can imagine."[28]

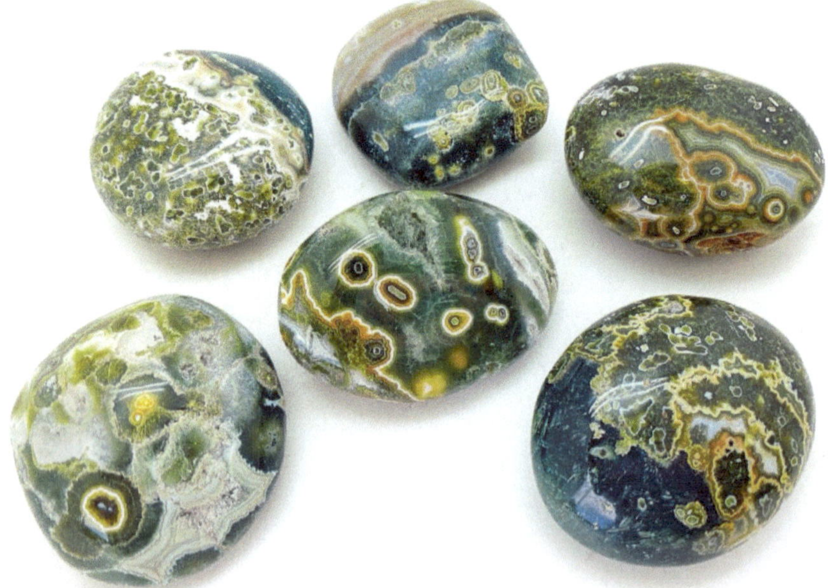

Fig. 14. Jasper. Wikimedia commons.

So, while it is not unusual to see images in these stones, it seems far more likely that Leonardo's motives were far more pragmatic. His notebooks reveal that he was a collector of fossils and stones and mentions the minerals diopside and jasper. At the time of the painting of the St. Anne, Leonardo was experimenting with mixtures of paints, allowing him to perfect a marbled or mottled appearance to his stones, Carlo Pedretti explains the process as follows. "Notebooks and sheets of about 1508 contain a number of notes on "mistioni" (mixtures) a plastic material of his own invention with which he aimed at imitating the colour and design of semi-precious stones. He describes his production process and how, once the objects were thus produced, he spent much time finishing them with his own hand to a smooth and glossy surface...At the same time he was much taken by anatomical studies, so that when he described the production process of his "mistioni" he came to specify the effect that was to be achieved: "...then you will dress it with peels of various colours, which will look like the mesentery of an animal". Two drawings of a mesentery in one of the anatomical studies at Windsor look remarkably like the decorative motif of his "mistioni". And it is no surprise, therefore, that the beautiful stone in the Louvre St. Anne should have been taken as an embryo."[29]

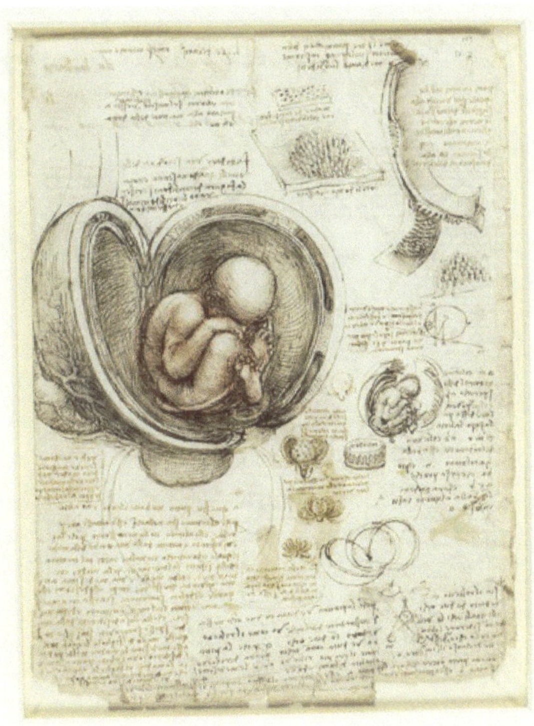

Fig. 15. An anatomical drawing by Leonardo of a fetus. Wikimedia commons.

Pedretti states that Leonardo was likely influenced by the vast collection of Medici gems, jewels and minerals.[30] The Medici collection was full of natural stones as well as those that had been incised and polished for use as jewelry. The reason why chalcedony, jasper, agates and other colorful stones have been used since antiquity for jewelry is because, when cut or buffed, they revealed combinations of patterns such as banding, dendritic forms or color variations which appeared to be a realistic scene or figure. In 1502, Francesco Malatesta wrote Isabella d'Este that Leonardo had looked at many of the Medici gems and objets d'art made of stone. Leonardo praised "the one of amethyst or jasper as Leonardo baptized it, because of the admirable rarity of its colors."[31]

Stones which are suited to intricate carving for emblems, crests and objets d'art are agates, onyx, chalcedony and varieties of quartz. We know that Leonardo prepared a sketch for an emblem, perhaps for someone in the Sforza court, entitled by Popham Allegory on the Fidelity of the Lizard,[32] this design would have been suitable for engraving onto a beautifully colored stone or incised on a medal.[34]

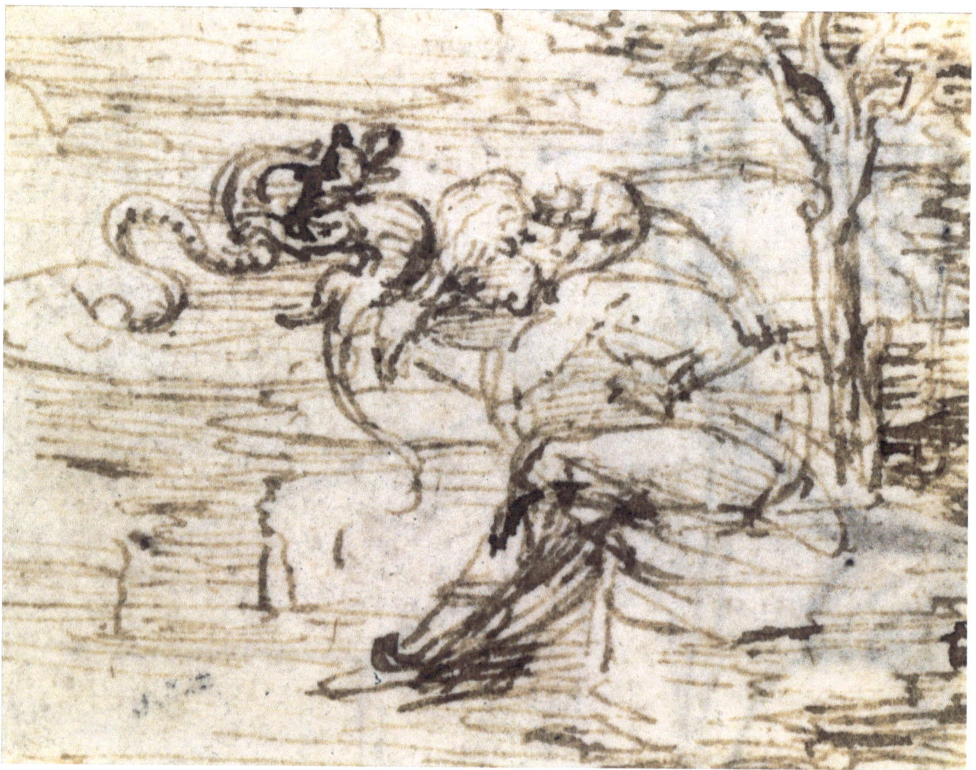

Fig. 16. Leonardo da Vinci, Allegory on the Fidelity of the Lizard 1496, Metropolitan Museum of Art, New York, Wikimedia commons.

Also, in the Windsor Castle Royal Library collection, is a design of St. John the Baptist which, in all likelihood was used as a model for an intaglio broach made of chalcedony entitled Diomede e il Palladio.[33]

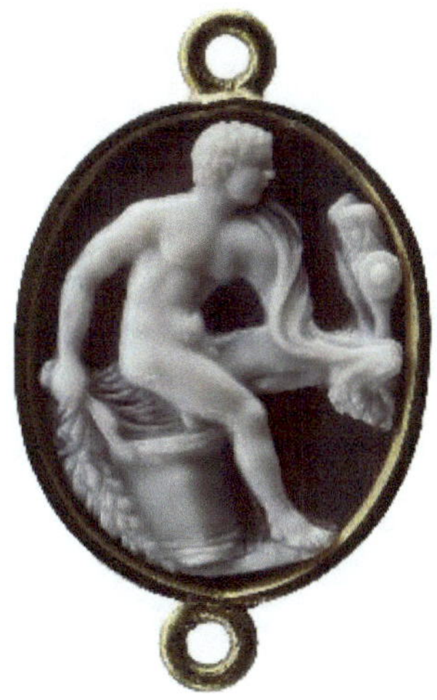

Fig. 17. The prototype of this cameo is surely the lost intaglio (design incised or engraved into a material) made of chalcedony by Dioskourides (late 1st century B.C. Roman gem-engraver) portraying Diomedes with the Palladion, which was part of the gem collection of Lorenzo the Magnificent. Wikimedia commons.

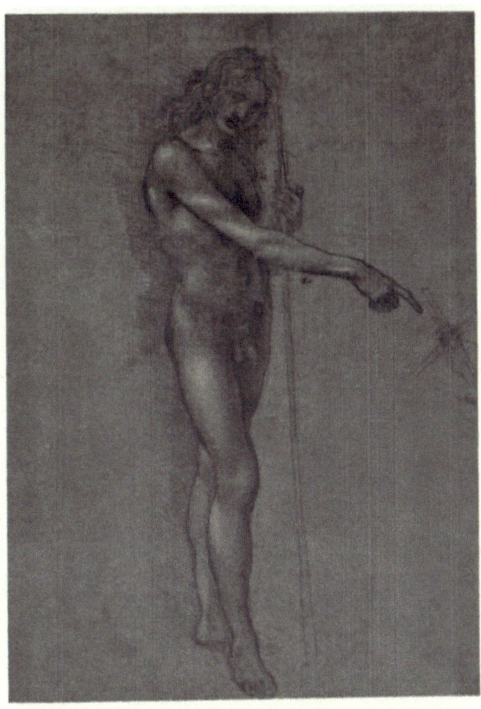

Fig. 18. Leonardo da Vinci, St. John the Baptist, World History Archive.

The geological complexity of the St. Anne demonstrates Leonardo's ongoing efforts to achieve an astounding level of sophistication not only in his portrayal of natural objects and figures but in his painting techniques as well. It is as if he struggled for so many years practicing the depiction of drapery, musculature and rock forms only to combine them with newly developed painting methods which allowed all of the elements to come together into a stunning creation. Perhaps the efforts of his entire life created, in the St. Anne, such a sense of beauty, mystery and empathy, that so many people with diverse backgrounds have felt compelled to comment on it. Whatever the mystique of the painting, it is truly one which presents the apex of a lifetime of study, experimentation and creativity.

# GLOSSARY

**agate**- variety of chalcedony forms from the deposition of silica in volcanic vesicles or other cavities. Impurities in the silica are responsible for bands of various colors.

**chalcedony**- A broad term to describe a microcrystalline form of silica composed of intergrowths of quartz (trigonal) and moganite (monoclinic) both have the same chemical composition $SiO_2$. There are a number of varieties: agate, chrysoprase, carnelian, heliotrope, moss agate and onyx.

**chrysoprase**- a green variety of chalcedony

**erosional remnants**- Any surface of rock or sediment whereby the motion of ice, water, wind or waves that has altered the surface and left behind evidence of such processes. glacial plain- Plains constructed by the direct action of the ice itself.

**heliotrope**- Green chalcedony containing red inclusions of iron oxide that resemble drops of blood (also known as bloodstone).

**jasper**- An aggregate of microgranular quartz and/or chalcedony is an impure variety of silica, usually red, yellow, brown or green. The red color comes from iron (III) inclusions.

**mature valley**- Mature valleys are wider, deeper and have gentler gradients and more and larger tributaries than young valleys. In early maturity they are roughly U-shaped, instead of V-shaped, as before. In late maturity they have conspicuous flats. These changes in cross section signify that down-cutting has come to be very slow, and that the processes which widen valleys and reduce their sides have become much more important relatively.

**mountain pediment**- A plain of combined erosion and transportation at the foot of a desert mountain range similar in form to the alluvial plains that front the mountains of an arid region, but without alluvial cover and composed of solid rock

**nunatuk**- The summit or the ridge of a mountain that protrudes from an ice field or glacier, they are angular or jagged.

**pinnacles**- Any high tower or spire-shaped pillar of rock, alone or cresting a summit. A tall slender, pointed mass; especially a lofty peak.

**pinnacle weathering**- Dissolution of a carbonate rock which results in removal of the more porous carbonate rock sometimes leaving pinnacles or chimneys to stand up in relief.

**scour**- Erosion, especially by moving water.

**scour and fill**- The process of cutting and refilling channels in sediments.

**scour depression**- Where the channel of a stream is curved, the swiftest thread of the current is near the outside of the bend. The maximum erosive force of the current is exerted over a crescentic area in the bend. These areas are likely to be scoured below the grade of the steam, producing the hollows here called scour depressions.

**terminal moraine**- Also called end moraine, forms at the snout (edge) of a glacier, marking its maximum advance. At this point, debris that has accumulated by plucking and abrasion, and has been pushed by the front edge of the ice, is driven no further and instead is dumped in a heap.

**travertine flowstone**- Calcium carbonate ($CaCO_3$), of light color and usually concretionary and compact, deposited from solution in groundwater and surface waters. Travertine flowstone results from water flowing over instead of dripping from a rock surface. This process deposits calcium carbonate which is saturated in the flowing water.

**valley glacier**- A glacier occupying a valley. mountain glacier; Alpine glacier.

# APPENDIX A
## Agate and Jasper

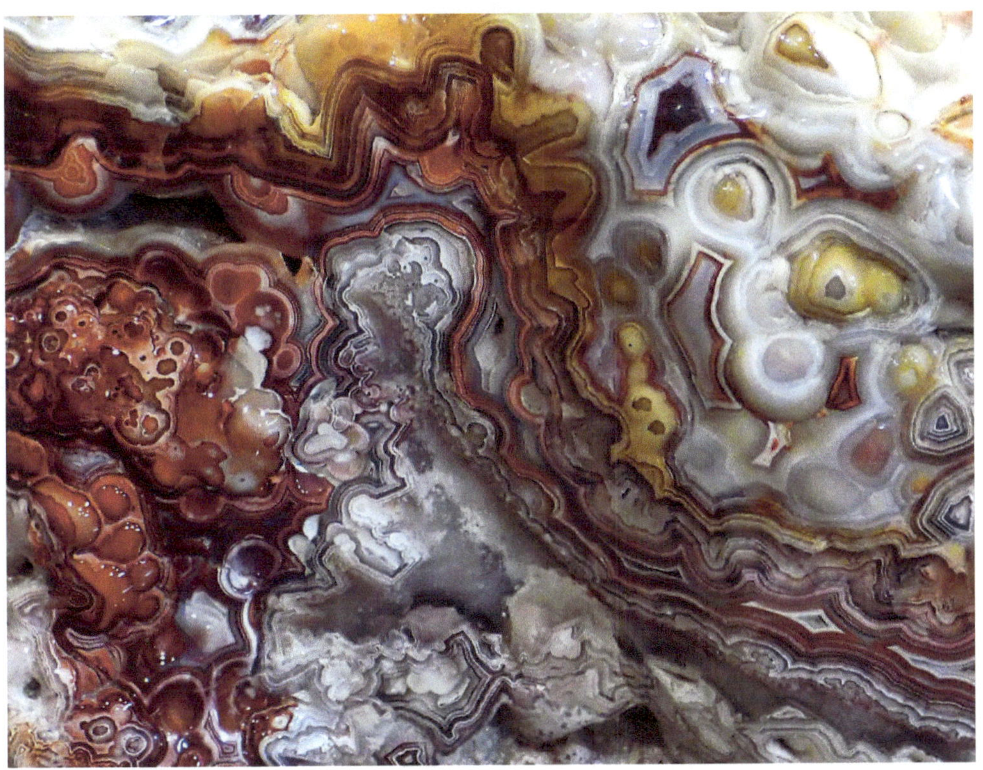

Agate. Wikimedia commons.

The pebbles we see beneath the feet of St. Anne and the Virgin were formed according to the principals of geochemistry. The parent rock is likely calcareous (i.e. limestone or dolomite) with agate lenses. Chalcedony is a broad term to describe a microcrystalline form of silica ($SiO2$). From this "parent", which is translucent, other variations are formed depending on the presence of other elements, which change the color and transparency. Jasper, for instance, is a type of chalcedony which is opaque, and due to the presence of iron(III) comes indifferent colors, usually red, yellow, brown or green.

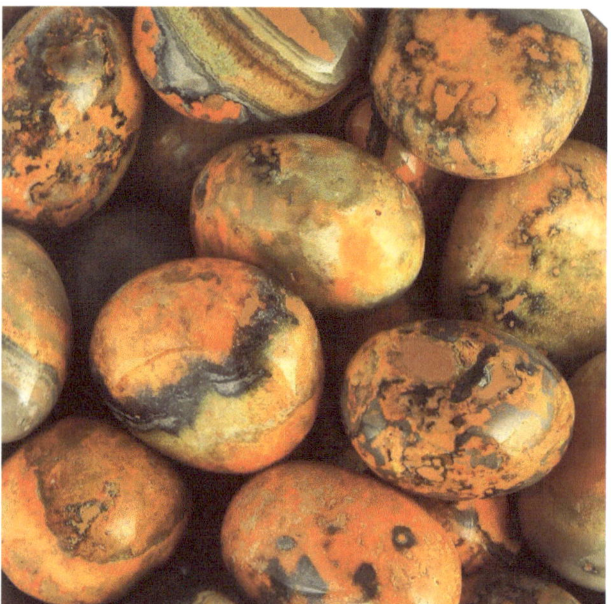

Jasper. Wikimedia commons.

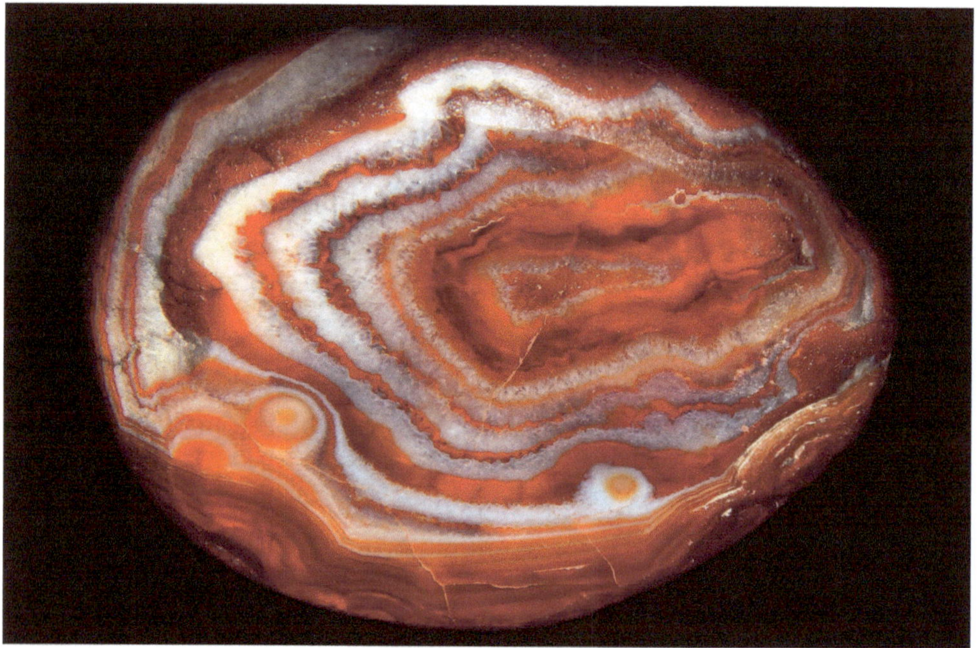

Agate. Wikimedia commons.

The banded layers of microscopic quartz colors which are found in banded agate form when silica is deposited in volcanic vesicles or other cavities. They are also formed in sedimentary rocks, normally limestone or dolomite. The bands are formed when layers of silica rich waters, infused with different minerals, solidify, one layer above another, forming beds of different colors. The development of varieties of chalcedony include onyx, chyrsoprase (a green variety), carnelian (red), heliotrope (green and containing red inclusions of iron oxide which resemble drops of blood, hence the common name "bloodstone") and moss agate (included minerals of manganese or iron form filaments and patterns resembling moss and other real objects). Chalcedony can be found in weathered volcanic rocks but also in sedimentary ones.

# APPENDIX B
## Botany

In addition to his precise portrayal of geologic formations, Leonardo produced some of the most stunningly accurate drawings of plants. In fact, he was a pioneer in botanic representation. His use of flora in his paintings had a dual purpose; aesthetics and symbolism. His notebooks were a testament to his passion for botany. He noted the arrangement of leaves on a plant stem (phyllotaxis), the rings on tree trunks and the reaction of plants to sun, air and gravity. He even conducted the first research into what is known today as hydroponics, the method of growing plants without soil using an aqueous solution. The Codex Urbinas provides a wealth of information on his observations of trees and the proper techniques to be used in depicting them in paintings. Considering this, it was important to analyze the tree in the painting because, as of this writing, no one has identified its species. Thus, it might also provide useful information for those art historians who have expressed the opinion that Leonardo did not paint the tree.

A number of botanists were asked if it was possible to identify the species of the tree. They were provided site specific information on location, soil types (limestone, dolomite and volcanic material), as well as climate and altitude. They were able to determine it was a deciduous broad-leaved tree with a spreading canopy, and suggested the following possibilities: Fraxinus excelsior (common ash), Fraxinus ornus (flowering/manna ash), and Castanea sativa (sweet chestnut).

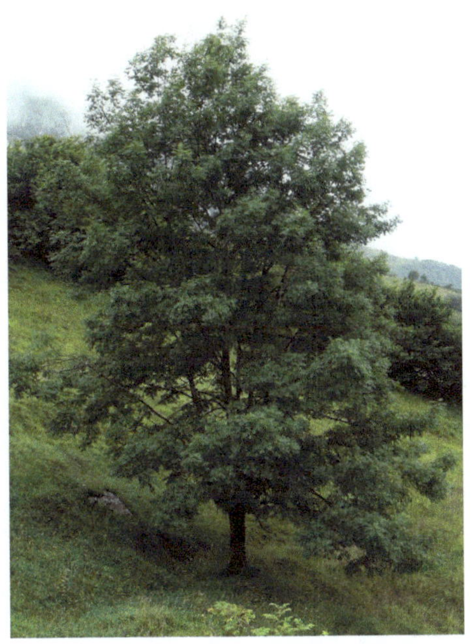

Fraxinus excelsior

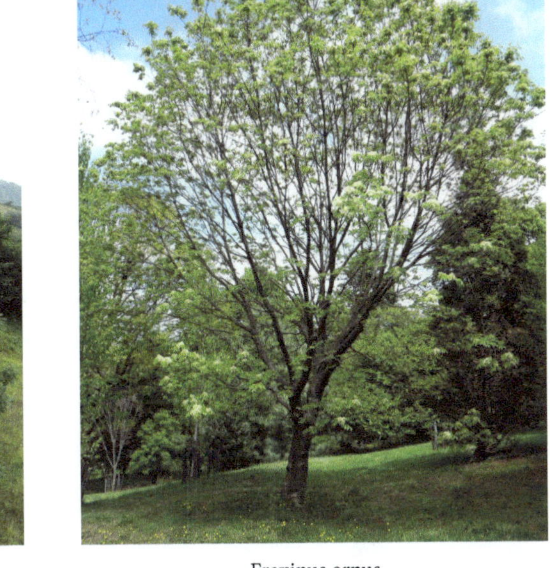

Fraxinus ornus

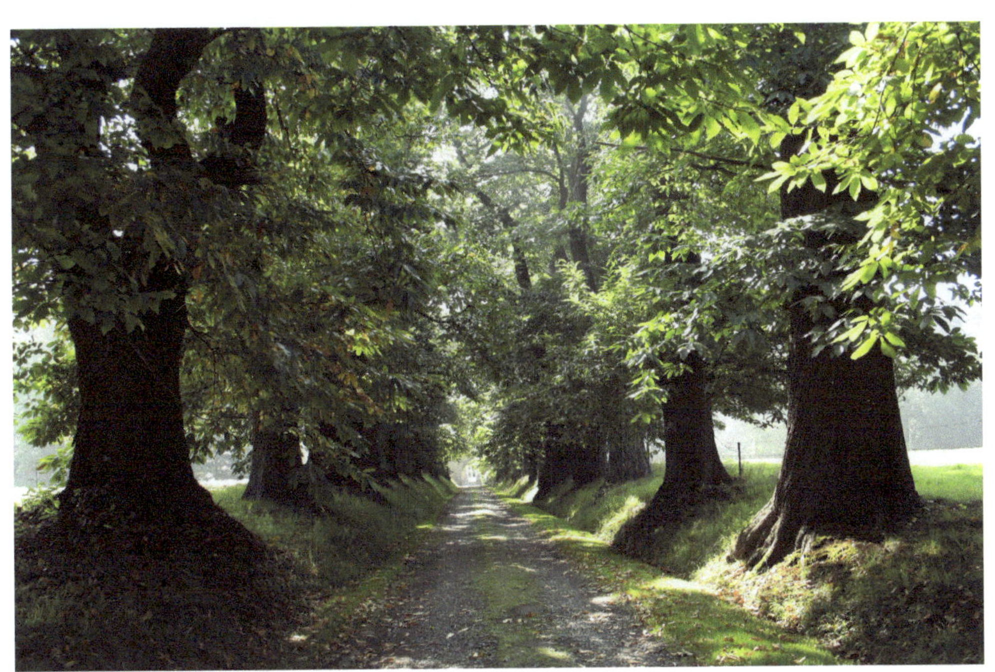

Castanea sativa

All photos: Wikimedia commons.

Various Italian botanical societies have compiled lists of the trees indigenous to the Dolomites. The predominant types are ash, oak and chestnut and grow in specific areas depending on variables such as altitude, soil conditions and sunlight. The three trees indicated by the botanists were present on the official botanic lists.

The botanists provided a number of cautionary notes, however. While the Fraxinus ornus (flowering/manna ash) grows in northern Italy, it would not attain high altitudes. This would either suggest that the tree would have to be eliminated from consideration or was growing in the valley between the crests (as could certainly be possibility, given the geomorphology of the area and its placement in the painting). The Castanea sativa (sweet chestnut) requires a mild climate and adequate moisture. Its year-growth (but not the rest of the tree) is sensitive to late spring and early autumn frosts (a possibility in high altitudes), and is intolerant of lime (which may be an issue if the terrain is limestone or dolomite). Its trunk is often 2 m. (7 ft.) in diameter (much too large to be the tree in the painting). While the leaves are appropriate for the Fraxinus excelsior (common ash) the tree's form might not be exact. However, this would not necessarily exclude it as a possibility, for a combination of growing patterns and artistic license could account for the more canopy-like growth at the top.

Once the possibilities were narrowed down, the choices were given to an artist to examine. The artist looked at actual photos and drawings of each of the trees, noting the leaf style and overall configuration including trunk, branches and autumnal leaf color changes. The artistic analysis is as follows. The chestnut was eliminated because, based on its form, the tree is too squat (chestnut trees can have a trunk diameter of over 2 m. or 7 ft.). The leaves and the branches are bunched together and thickly set (i.e. stubby). Also the leaves have a saw-tooth edge to them, unlike the smooth-edged elliptically formed Fraxinus (ash) leaves. The ash tree has leaves that are separated and are finer (thinner). The artistic effect, imparted by the slim and rapid brush strokes, gives the impression of delicacy, especially in the upper part of the tree where the leaves and their placement relative to one another on the branch are well defined. They are clearly depicted as pinnate compound leaves (A leaf which is divided into smaller leaflets, those leaflets arranged on each side of the leaf's central stalk/rachis (axis)). Considering that the tree is in the background, it would have been impossible for Leonardo to have given a single leaf more defining characteristics, as that would have ruined the perspective. The silhouette of the tree as well as the shape of the leaves resembles and ash.

When painting groups of plants, the shape of the leaves, stems, petals and branches must be unique enough to identify the plant while maintaining realism. If the florae are in the distance, too highly detailed identifying characteristics would ruin the authentic feel of the painting. This is called "gesture drawing". The form is what strikes the eye and gives one a sense of realism. Since the tree is about 40 meters away from the figures, it would be impossible to identify the detail in a single leaf. Considering the mass of the tree's foliage, one would have to be guided by the form and silhouette.

As for the color of the tree, Leonardo's primary concern was to create a cohesive color assemblage. Since the background mountains were gray-white and blue-gray and the foreground rocks were coppery red, he had to choose a hue for the tree which would coordinate with the color scheme and provide unity in the painting. He chose to paint the tree coppery brown, which is the color of ash trees in the autumn. However, in choosing the tonality, he had to consider how far away the tree was from the viewer as well as the atmospheric conditions which might affect how it would be seen. For instance, he had to consider environmental (ambient) light. It seems that the tree is against the light, because the leaves at the top seem to be reflecting the sunlight and thus appear more yellow, while the foliage in the center appears almost black because it is in the shade and appears to be backlit. These are the primary three reasons for the tonality we see; distance, light and palette.

We must also consider the difficulty in obtaining and preparing the exact color Leonardo wanted for the tree. Whatever the original color was, they can change appearance in 500 years. They might have had a different tonality, sfumatura (shading) and brilliance when they were first used. Layers of varnish and/or glaze also covered the painting, applied either by Leonardo, restorers, or both. Finally, it was cleaned in 2011, changing the color and perhaps removing details.

With the artistic and botanical analysis in hand, the Castanea sativa (oak) tree was eliminated from consideration mainly because of its thick-bodied form. Fraxinus ornus (flowering/manna ash) remained in consideration, but because it grows at lower levels and remnants of its abundant flowers might be present on the tree, impacting its aesthetic form, it would not be the first choice. The Fraxinus excelsior (common ash) fits all the criteria botanically and artistically, so it would be the first choice as the tree depicted in the painting.

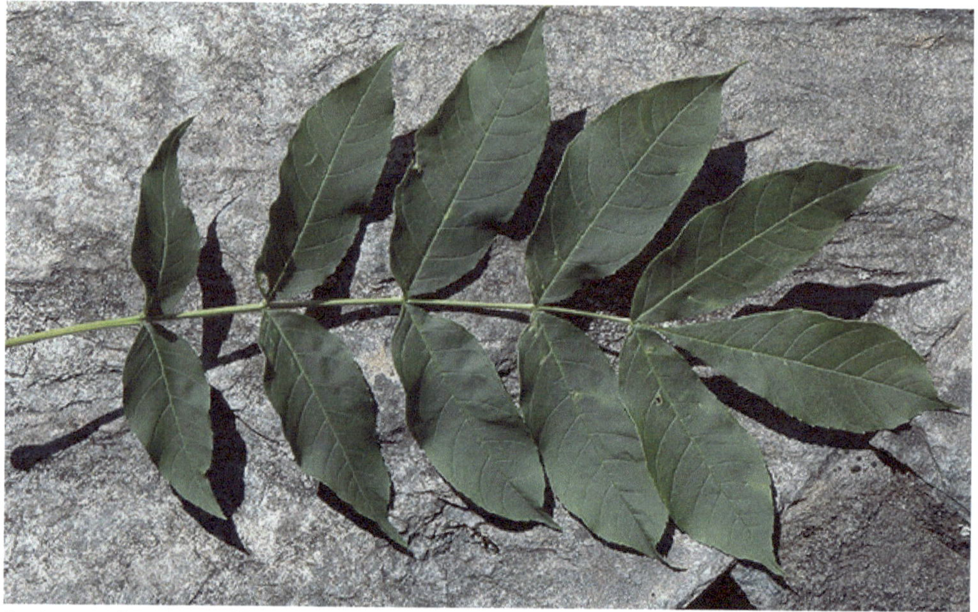

Fraxinus excelsior stem and leaves. Wikimedia commons.

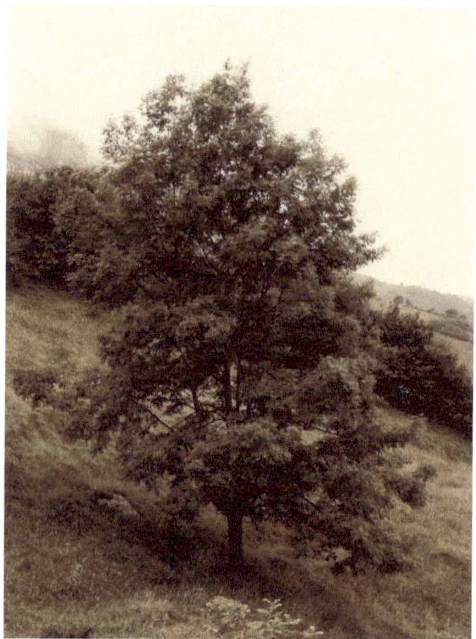

Fraxinus excelsior (common ash).
Wikimedia commons.

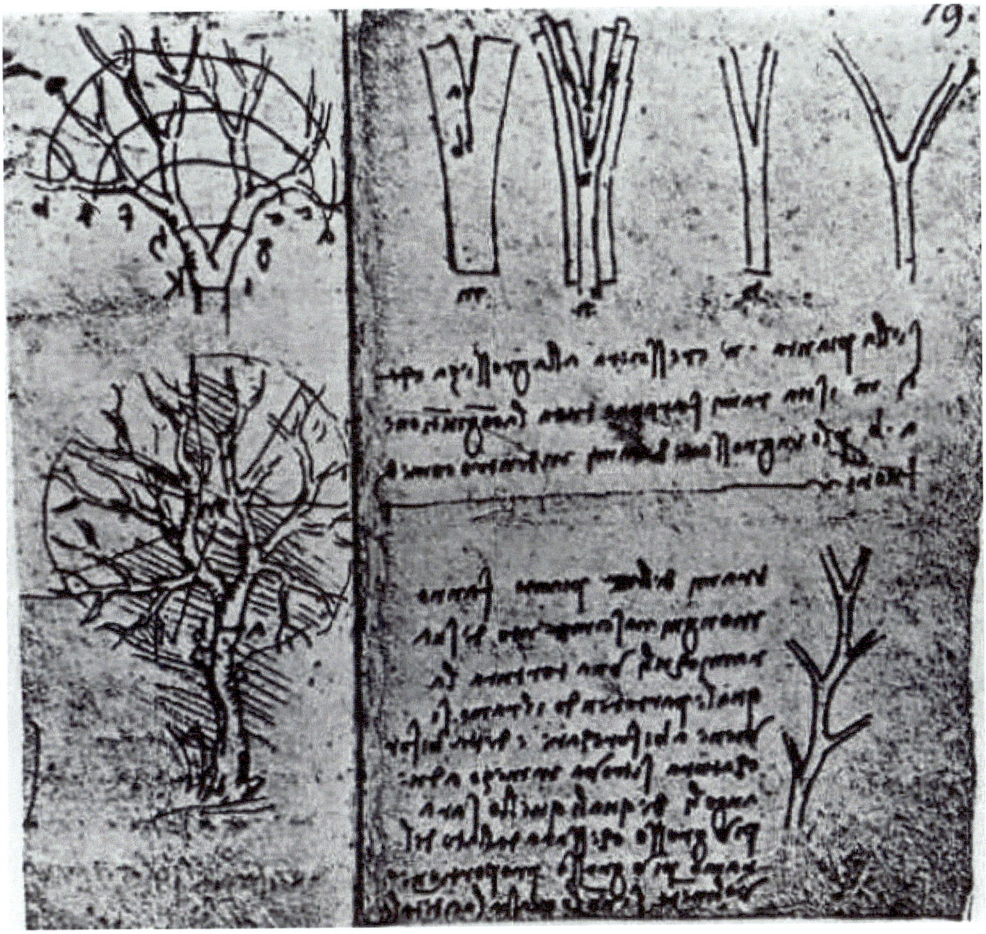

Leonardo's sketches and notes on the structure of trees. He also gives instructions on how to paint them considering light, distance and atmospheric conditions. Wikimedia.

Leonardo da Vinci, designs of bark and branch configurations in three types of trees: hazelnut, elder and elm. Wikimedia.

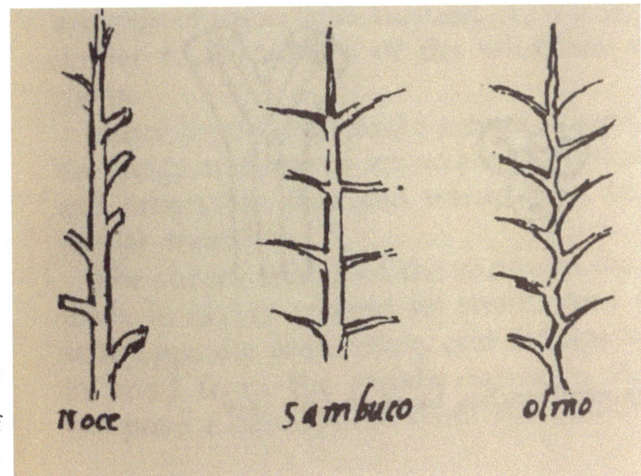

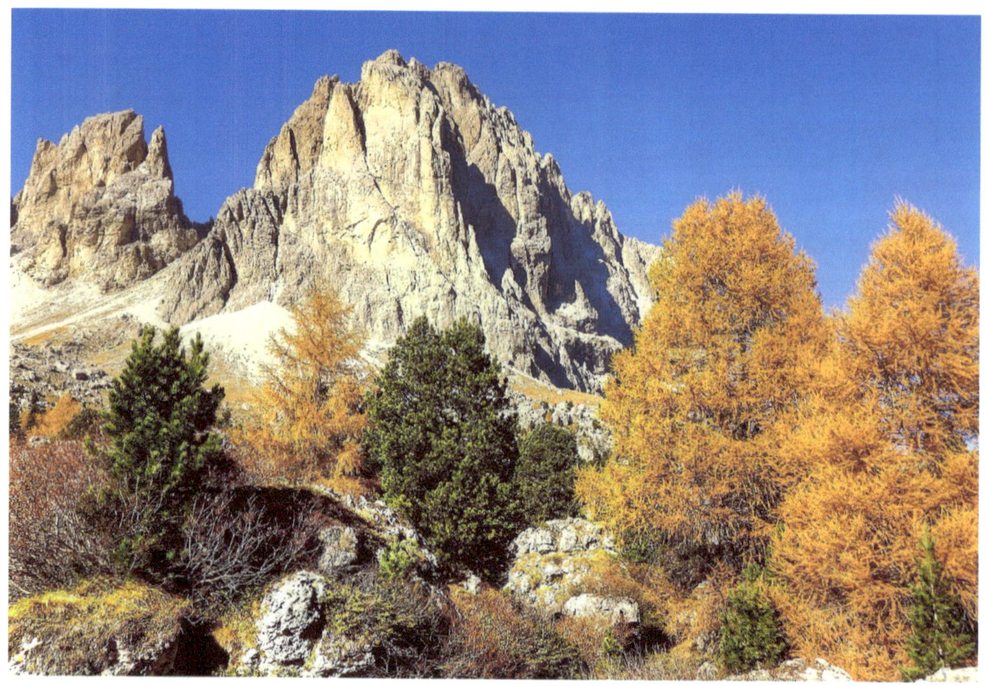

Dolomite landscape with indigenous trees.

# APPENDIX C
## The Geology of the Dolomites

The Dolomites are mountains in the southern Alps straddling the borders of three Italian provinces: South Tyrol, Trentino and Belluno. Because of their astounding beauty and geological/cultural uniqueness, they were declared a UNESCO World Heritage site in 2009. These mountains exist in an area which was much different during the Triassic Period (circa 250 million years ago) when the ancient tropical Tethys Ocean, replete with coral reefs and interspersed with volcanic constructs, covered the exact same location. The Tethys Ocean divided the African and Eurasian tectonic plates, but when they collided (circa 20 million years ago), forming the Alps, the Tethys disappeared and its oceanic sediments were lithified upon burial then pushed upward, forming the Dolomites.

The predominant stone of the mountains is dolostone which consists of the mineral dolomite, an anhydrous carbonate mineral [$CaMg(CO_3)_2$] formed from the fossilized coral reefs and adjacent sedimentary strata deposited in the Tethys Ocean. Since there was ongoing volcanic activity in and around the Tethys, volcanic material was continually intermixed with the coral reef strata. As a result, volcanic rocks are found in the Dolomites today. Part of the Dolomites' beauty is the abrupt change between towering rugged peaks and hilly green mountain pastures. This is due, in part, to the distinct hardness of various rocks resulting from different rates of erosion. Occurring over millions of years, the effects of earthquakes, volcanoes, ice, wind, flooding and elevation fluctuations developed a sculpted landscape replete with pinnacles, table mountains, and massifs punctuated with meadows.

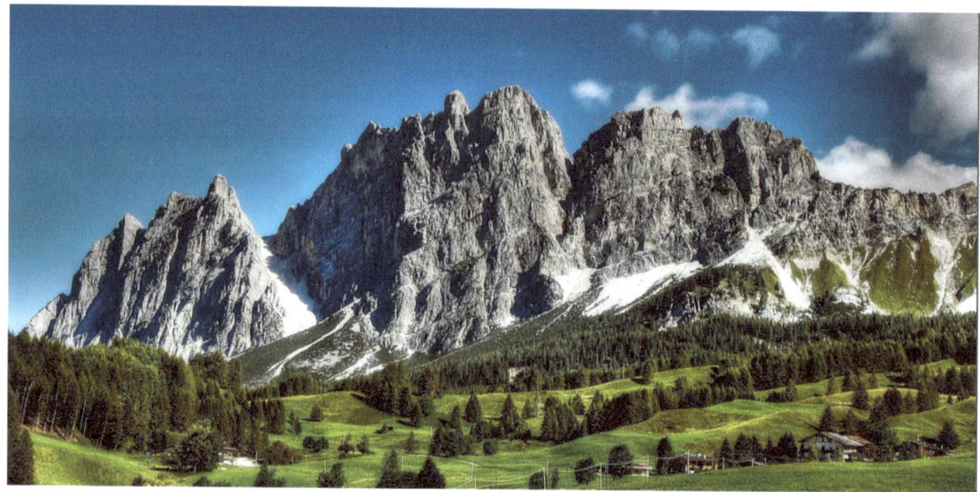

Dolomites landscape.

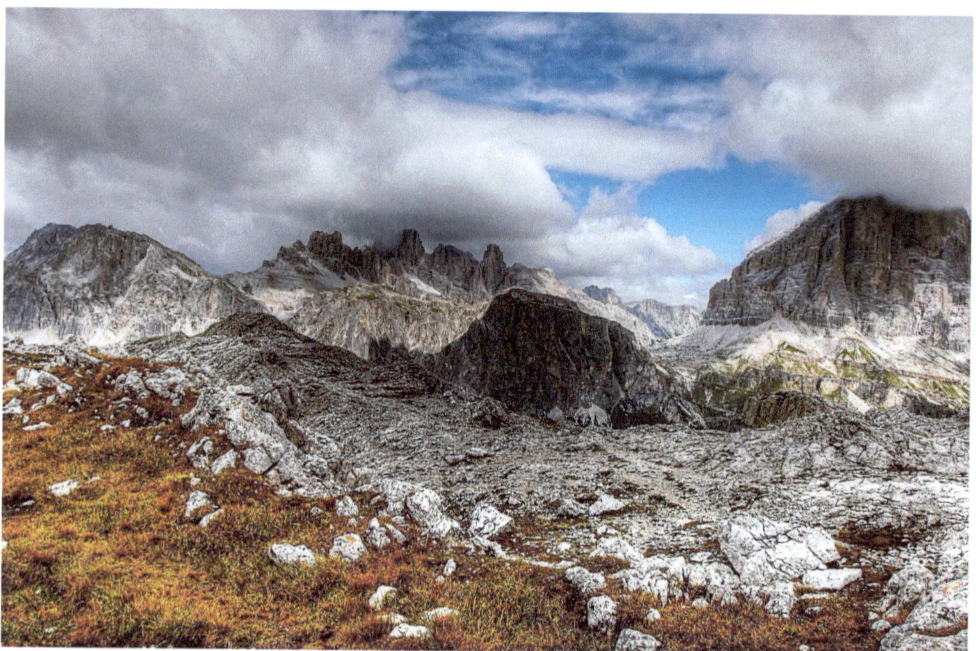

Dolomites landscape.

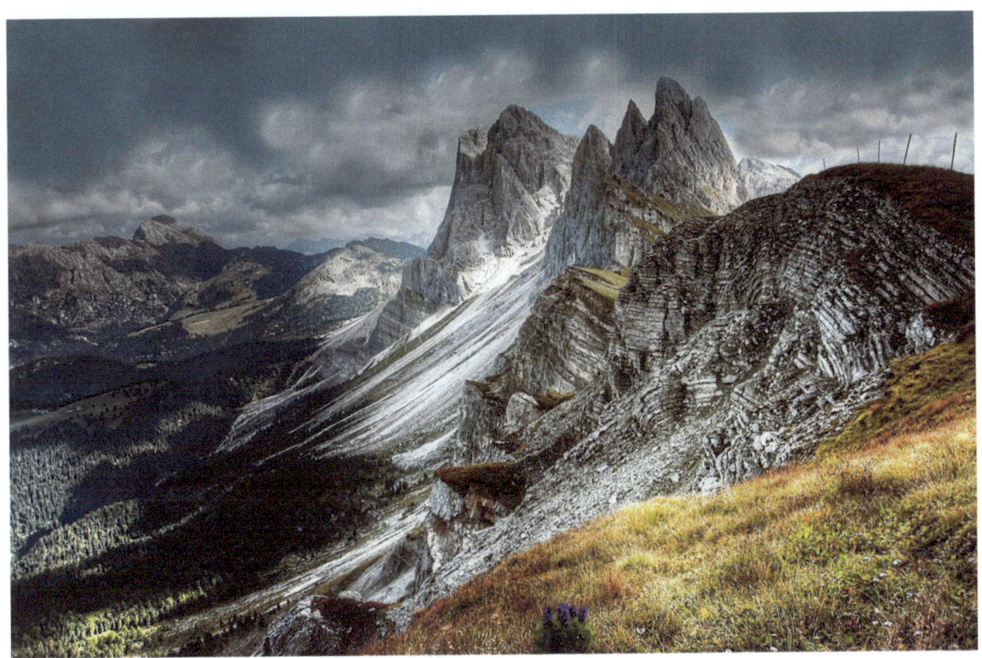

Dolomites landscape.

# APPENDIX D
## Freud And The Virgin And Child And St. Anne

In Freud's monograph, Leonardo da Vinci and a Memory of His Childhood* (1910) he constructs a psychoanalytic profile of the artist based on one quote in the Codex Atlanticus, where Leonardo recounts being attacked by a bird as an infant in his crib. "It seems that it had been destined before that I should occupy myself so thoroughly with the vulture, for it comes to my mind as a very early memory, when I was still in the cradle, a vulture came down to me, he opened my mouth with his tail and struck me a few times with his tail against my lips." (Italics added for emphasis) Freud, taking this quote as exact (it was not, as will be shown) declared this was Leonardo's childhood dream, based on a perceived memory of sucking his mother's nipple. He bolstered this claim by citing Egyptian hieroglyphic images depicting the mother as a vulture-headed goddess with a body resembling a phallus but with female breasts.

Unfortunately, Freud's psychoanalytic conjectures were futile, as they were based on a mistaken German translation (from the original Italian). In 1904, Mariz Herzfeld translated the Italian word nibbio as geier meaning vulture. In fact, the word nibbio means kite, a small hawk-like bird of prey found in Tuscany (the German word for kite is milan). This error was not discovered until after Freud's publication of the work in 1910.

In the same monograph, Freud went on to analyze the iconography in the painting. He proposed the idea that the Virgin and St. Anne represented Leonardo's two mothers. Leonardo had been born illegitimate, living near his real mother in his paternal grandfather's home until age 5 and then with his father and his wife (a different woman) thereafter. So, Freud felt that Leonardo, depicting two women whose age difference was minimal, was paying tribute to the women who raised him.

* This is a brief explanation of those issues which concern the historical comments regarding the St. Anne. The monograph discusses other aspects of Leonardo's life and work, but are beyond the scope of this commentary. For a full discussion, the book is available online.

After the second edition of the work was released, Oskar Pfister, a Swiss Lutheran minister and lay psychoanalyst, discovered, in 1919, the outline of a vulture in the garments of the Virgin (it actually looks more like a duck but bears no resemblance to a kite). The image of the outline of a "vulture" in the clothing was included in subsequent editions of Freud's book.

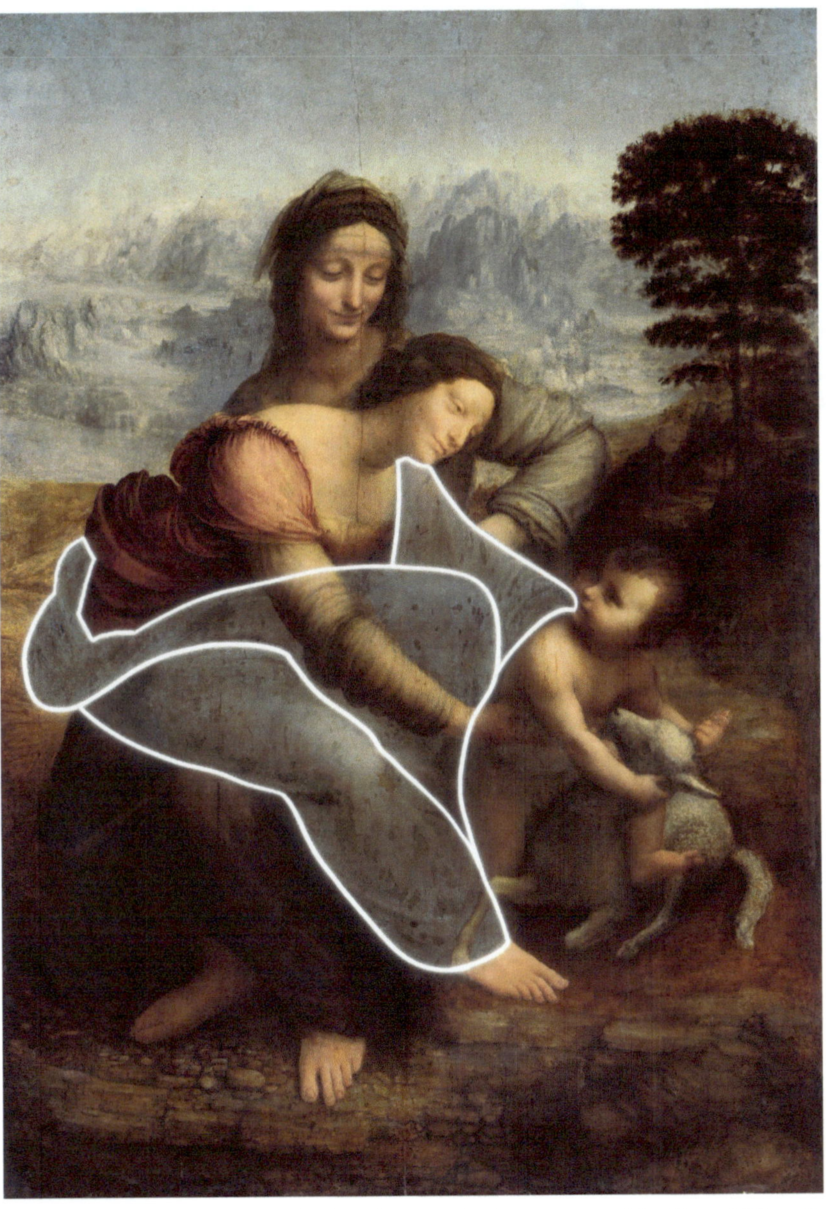

Diagram of the "vulture" imagined to have been seen in the vestments of the Virgin. Wikimedia

Once the translation error was discovered, Freud was criticized and became disillusioned. He confessed to Lou Andreas-Salomé in a letter of February 9, 1919, that he regarded the Leonardo essay as "the only beautiful thing I have ever written".

# APPENDIX E
## Leonardo And The Natural World

Throughout his life, Leonardo paid special attention to nature in all its manifestations: rocks, plants, water and air. He wrote and sketched as he traveled, thus memorializing many of the unique geologic formations and plants he saw. In fact, his paintings show such a remarkable fidelity to nature that geologists can identify the rock formations and botanists the plants. In prior publications, this author analyzed the geology and botany in the two versions of the Virgin of the Rocks (one in the Louvre and one in the National Gallery in London). The painting in the Louvre shows a remarkable fidelity to nature, while the rocks and plants in the London version are not accurate.

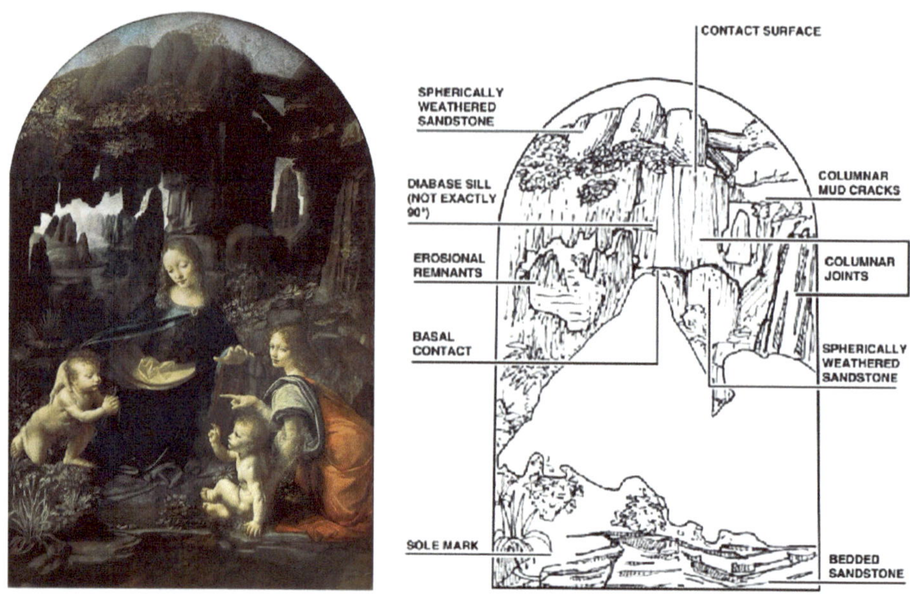


Left: Leonardo da Vinci, Virgin of the Rocks, 1483-86, Louvre, Paris, Wikimedia. Right: Geologic detail. © Ann C. Pizzorusso 2021.

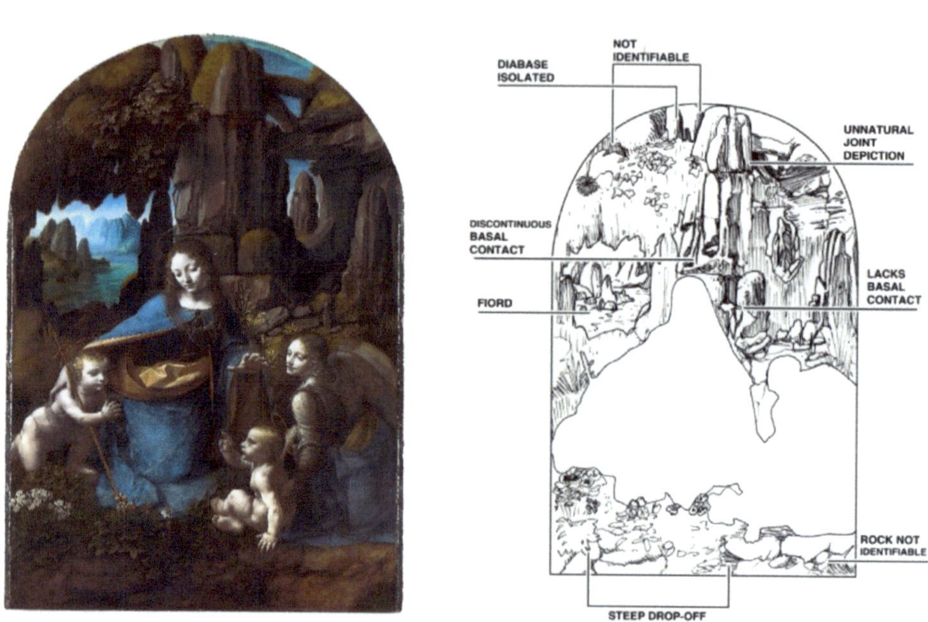


Left: Leonardo da Vinci, Virgin of the Rocks, between circa 1491 and circa 1499 and from 1506 until 1508, National Gallery, London, Wikimedia. Right: geologic detail. © Ann C. Pizzorusso 2021.

Leonardo also imparted his respect for nature to his students Marco D'Oggiono and Antonio Boltraffio. Their painting, the Resurrection, in Berlin shows rock formations depicted with the utmost care. While the painters lacked the talent of Leonardo, the geologic formations in the painting are accurate enough to be identified. The influence of their teacher is in evidence.

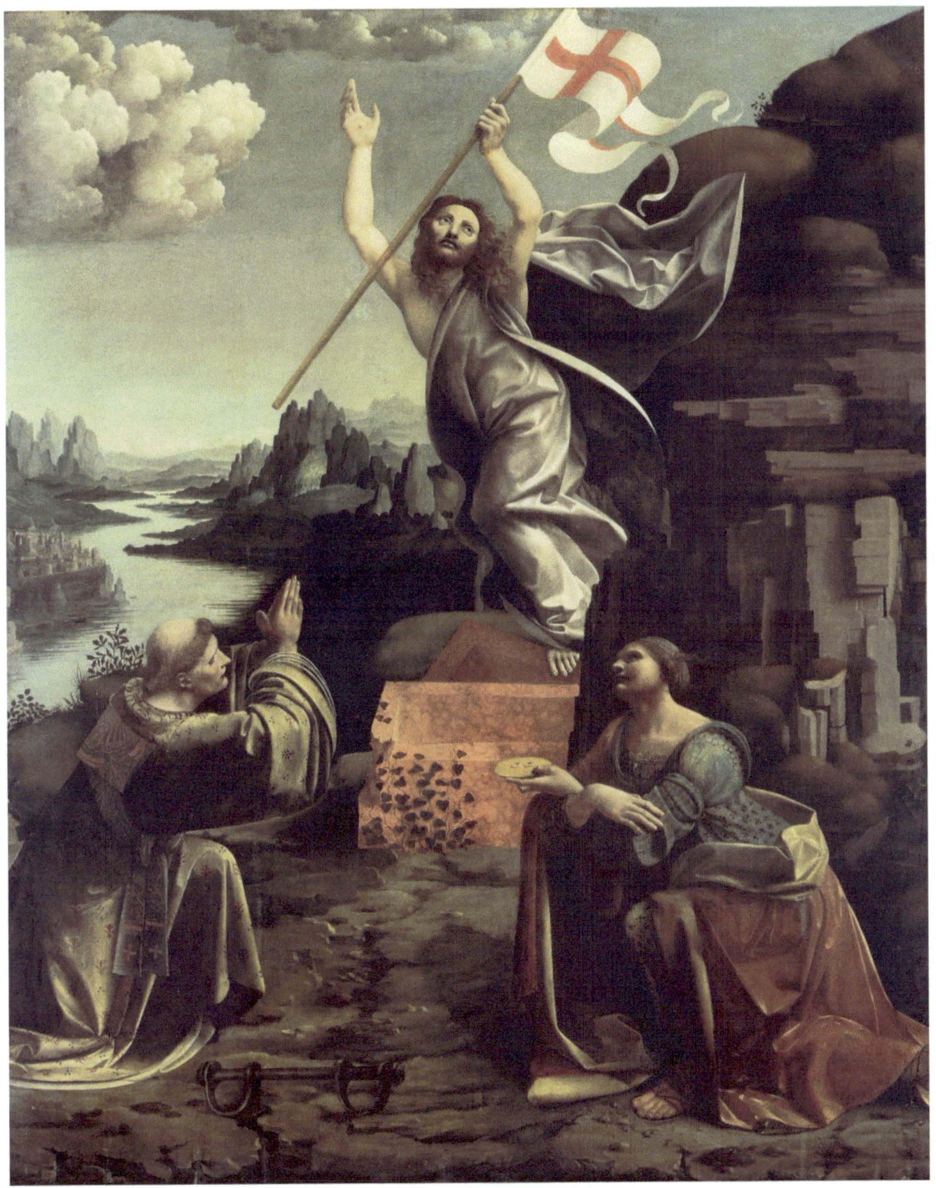

Boltraffio and d'Oggiono, Resurrection, 1491. Gemäldegalerie der Staatlichen Museen zu Berlin. Wikimedia.

Leonardo's interest in the geomorphic configuration of the terrain led him to become an expert cartographer. He developed the technique of a "bird's eye view" of the land, leading to the most extraordinarily accurate (and beautiful) maps ever created. With his artistic skill, he was able to impart a sense of three-dimensionality to his maps, using hyposometric color to define the relative height of hills and mountains as well as the depth of water.

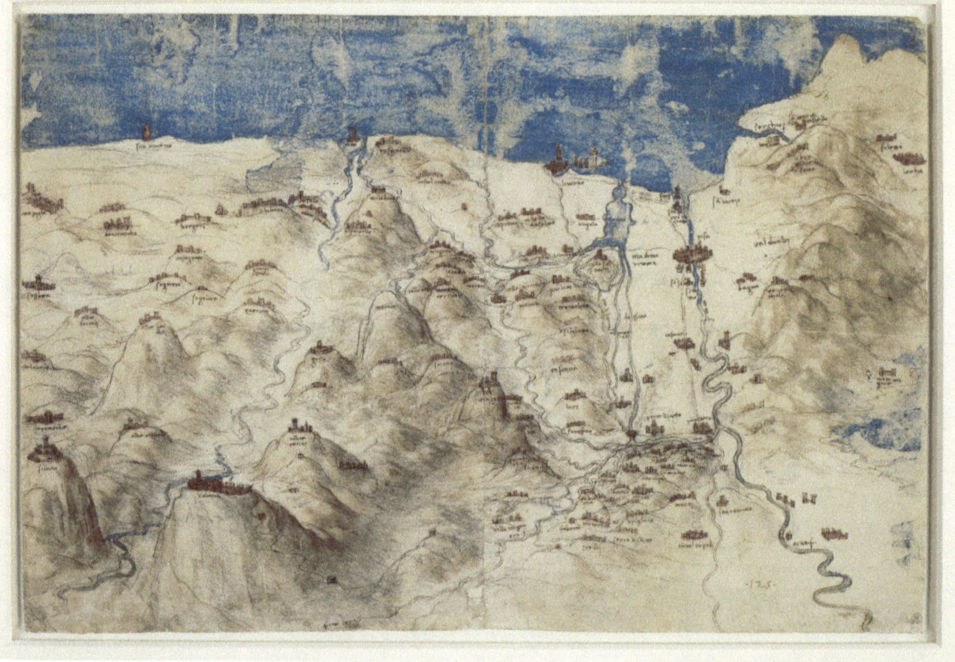

Leonardo da Vinci, Map of Tuscany. The Royal Collection © Her Majesty Queen Elizabeth II 2020.

His accurate depiction of plants in his paintings can be attributed to an unerring eye and an enduring curiosity about botany. His notebooks and sketches provide insight into his astute observations about plant structure and growth. They are so sophisticated that a modern botanist can understand his scientific observations.

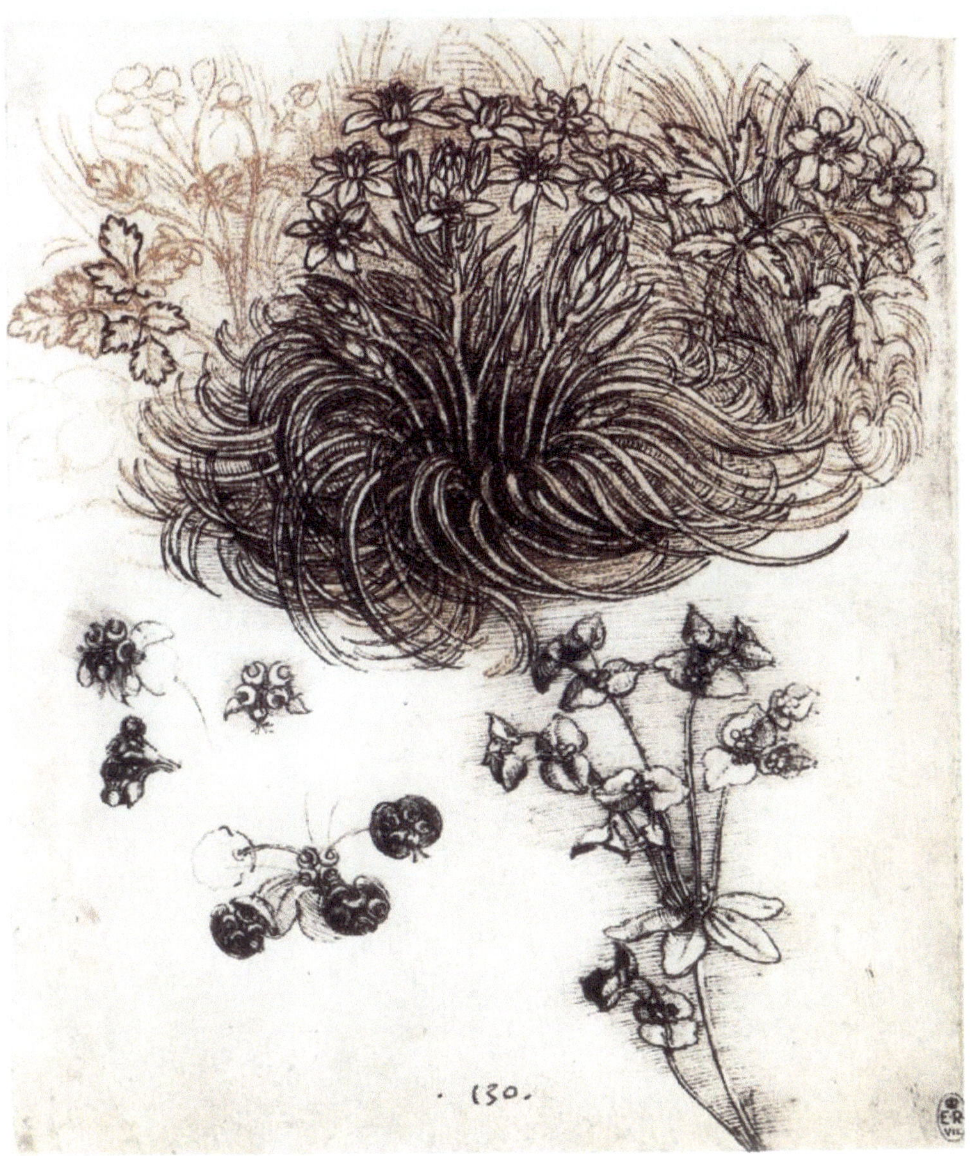

Leonardo da Vinci, Star of Bethlehem, wood anemone and sun spurge, 1505-10,
The Royal Collection © Her Majesty Queen Elizabeth II 2020.

# ACKNOWLEGEMENTS

Many thanks to all the experts who have so graciously spent their time reviewing this book. Their comments and observations helped to make this work the best it could be. The challenge in preparing a multi-disciplinary work is to find and reach out to experts in many fields. Leonardo da Vinci was able to do it alone, but the process of interpreting his work involves the cooperation of many accomplished scholars: Charles Merguerian, geologist, Jacques Franck, art historian, Michael C. Daley, art historian, Matthew Hall, botanist and Faith Douglas, botanist. Also, to the talented artist who created the cover and designs in the book, Francesco Filippini. And finally, Giuseppe De Matola for daily inspiration

# ABOUT THE AUTHOR

Ann C. Pizzorusso is a geologist and Italian Renaissance scholar. After many years of doing virtually everything in the world of geology—drilling for oil, hunting for gems, cleaning up pollution in soil and groundwater, she turned her geologic skills toward Leonardo da Vinci. In addition to many scholarly articles, she is the author of the multi- prize winning book Tweeting da Vinci (Twittando da Vinci, Italian edition) and Leonardo da Vinci Cartographer and Inventor of the Google Map.

# BIBLIOGRAPHY


1.Bean, Jacob, Fifteenth and Sixteenth Century Italian Drawings in the Metropolitan Museum of Art, New York, 1982.

2.Beck, James, Italian Renaissance Painting, Harper and Row, New York, 1981.

3. Boussel, Patrice, Leonardo da Vinci, Chartwell, Seacaucus, NJ., 1992.

4.Clark, Kenneth, Leonardo da Vinci, Penguin, London, 1998.

5.Da Vinci, Leonardo, John, R; Don Read, J (eds.). Note-Books Arranged And Rendered Into English, Empire State Book Co., 1923.

6.Dacos, Nicole, Il Tesoro di Lorenzo il Magnifico, volume primo, Le Gemme, Sansoni, Firenze, 1972.

7. Da Vinci, Leonardo, John, R; Don Read, J (eds.) Note-Books Arranged and Rendered into English, Empire State Book Co. New York, NY. 1923.

8.Franck, Jacques, "Léonard de Vinci, De la Sainte Anne de Londres à la Sainte Anne du Louvre: le véritable déroulement d'une création." ArtItalies, la revue de l'AHAI, n. 25, 2019, p.122-138.

9.Freud, Sigmund, Leonardo da Vinci and a Memory of his Childhood, W.W. Norton & Co., New York, 1964.

10.McCurdy, Edward, The Notebooks of Leonardo da Vinci, Arcturus Publishing, London, 2017.

11.Ottino della Chiesa, Angela, The Complete Paintings of Leonardo da Vinci, Penguin, New York, 1967.

12.Pedretti, Carlo, Leonardo, A Study in Chronology and Style, London, 1974. 13.Pizzorusso, Ann, Leonardo's Geology: The Authenticity of the Virgin of the Rocks, in

Leonardo Magazine, vol. 29, no. 3, MIT Press, 1996.

14.Richter, Irma A., The Notebooks of Leonardo da Vinci, Oxford University Press, Oxford, 1980

15.Stites, Raymond S., The Sublimations of Leonardo da Vinci, Washington, 1970.

Websites: Dolomites trees: http://dryades.units.it/dolomitibellunesi/index.php?procedure=taxon_page&id=3975&nu m=21https://www.dolomitiparco.com/Materiali/Testi/Atlante-floristico.pdf La Flora delle Dolomiti, http://www.dolomitiunesco.it/le-dolomiti/la-flora/

# FOOTNOTES

1. Jacques Franck, "Léonard de Vinci, De la Sainte Anne de Londres à la Sainte Anne du Louvre: le

véritable déroulement d'une création." ArtItalies, la revue de l'AHAI, n. 25, 2019, p.122-138. 2. Patrice Boussel, Leonardo da Vinci (Chartwell, Seacaucus, N.J., 1992), pg. 27.

3. Sigmund Freud, Leonardo da Vinci and a Memory of his Childhood (New York, 1964), pg. 72. See also Appendix D

4.Stites, Raymond S., The Sublimations of Leonardo da Vinci, Smithsonian Institution Press Washington, D.C., pg. 170.

5. Patrice Boussel, Leonardo da Vinci (Chartwell, Seacaucus, N.J., 1992), pg. 27.

6.Leonardo's accurate portrayal of geologic formations was his trademark. For a discussion on Leonardo's geologic accuracy in his paintings and drawings, see Ann Pizzorusso, Leonardo's Geology: The Authenticity of the Virgin of the Rocks in Leonardo Magazine, Vol. 29, No. 3, 1996, pp.197-200. MIT Press. Also Appendix E.

7. Leonardo's notebooks cover a myriad of geologic disciplines. He wrote and sketched, among other things, ideas about stratigraphy, paleontology, structural geology, hydrology and geomorphology.

8.Codex Urbinas Latinus 1270 144v.-145r. states "The lower contours of distant objects will be less discernable than their upper contours, and this occurs especially with mountains and hills, the summits of which have as their background the sides of other mountains which are behind them. And in these, the upper contours are seen more readily than their bases, because the upper contour is darker on account of its being less covered by the thick air which is low-lying, and which indeed obscures the aforesaid contours of the bases of the hills..."

9.Leonardo da Vinci, Manuscripts of France, Ms. Ashburnham II, BN 2038 25r.

10.Leonardo da Vinci, Codex Urbinas Latinus,33v.-34r.v. (Boticelli) "And such painter made very poor landscapes." (lu 60) McM 93)

11.Ibid.

12.Carlo Pedretti, Leonardo, A Study in Chronology and Style, (London, 1974), p. 128.

13.James Beck, Italian Renaissance Painting, (New York, 1981), p. 300.

14. Ann Pizzorusso, 'Leonardo's Geology: The Authenticity of the Virgin of the Rocks' in Leonardo Magazine, Vol. 29, No. 3, 1996, pp. 197-200.

15. Leonardo da Vinci, Nature Studies from the Royal Library at Windsor Castle Catalogue by Carlo Pedretti, Introduction by Kenneth Clark, p. 9.

16.Angela Ottino della Chiesa, The Complete Paintings of Leonardo da Vinci (New York, 1967), p. 108. 17.Kenneth Clark, Leonardo da Vinci, (New York, 1988) p. 213.

18.James Beck, Italian Renaissance Painting, (New York, 1981), p. 30419. Kenneth Clark, Leonardo da Vinci, (London, 1988), p. 213.

19.Kenneth Clark, Leonardo da Vinci, (New York, 1988) p. 213.

20.Carlo Pedretti, Leonardo, A Study of Chronology and Style, (London, 1974), p. 129.

21.Carlo Pedretti, Leonardo, A Study of Chronology and Style, (London, 1974), p. 129.

22. Ibid.

23.See Apendix A

24.Ann Pizzorusso and an artist examined the area and find no evidence of a pool of water at the feet of the Virgin and St. Anne.

25.Raymond Stites, The Sublimation of Leonardo da Vinci, (Washington, 1970), p. 307. and 397 26. Ibid pg. 397

27.The notebooks of Leonardo da Vinci, MS 2038, Bib. Nat. 22v. McCurdy, 1906 pg. 173. 28.Carlo Pedretti, Leonardo, A Study in Chronology and Style, (London, 1974), p. 135.

29. Carlo Pedretti, Leonardo, A Study in Chronology and Style, (London, 1974), p. 132. 30.Carlo Pedretti, Leonardo, A Study in Chronology and Style, (London, 1974), p. 137. 31.Nicole Dacos, Il Tesoro di Lorenzo il Magnifico, (Florence, 1972), p. 127

32. Jacob Bean, Fifteenth and Sixteenth Century Italian Drawings at the Metropolitan Museum of Art, (New York, 1982), p. 11833.Nicole Dacos, Il Tesoro di Lorenzo il Magnifico, (Florence, 1972), p. 160.